Eerie Companions:
A History of Haunted Dolls

David Weatherly
Eerie Lights Publishing

Eerie Companions:
A History of Haunted Dolls

Based on interviews and research
conducted by David Weatherly

ISBN 978-1-945950-05-6 (Paperback)

EERIE LIGHTS

EERIE LIGHTS PUBLISHING
Nevada

Also by David Weatherly

Black Eyed Children

Strange Intruders

Eerie Companions: A History of Haunted Dolls

Silver State Monsters: Cryptids & Legends of Nevada

Copper State Monsters: Cryptids & Legends of Arizona

The Haunted Series (co-authored with Ross Allison)

Haunted Toys

Haunted Ships & Lighthouses

Haunted Churches

Shadow Chaser (co-authored with Sean Austin)

Wood Knocks: A Journal of Sasquatch Research

Volume One

Volume Two

Volume Three

Table of Contents

Acknowledgements

As with any project of this depth, there are plenty of people to thank for direct assistance and general support.

First and foremost, thanks to everyone who shared stories of haunted dolls as well as their thoughts and opinions. Additionally, it's always good to have colleagues like Rosemary Ellen Guiley, John Zaffis and Ross Allison who have also dealt with haunted objects over the years.

Thanks also to Ross for the intro to Mr. Creepy and the other haunted dolls at his Seattle museum.

Thanks to my friend Chad Lewis who came in with a last-minute pic of Robert the Doll since my own photos proved difficult to locate. I suspect it's due to Robert up to his standard mischief.

Special thanks to Zak Bagans for access to the creepy doll collection at his Haunted Museum in Las Vegas, use of the Annabelle photo, and discussions about his experiences with haunted and possessed dolls.

Thanks to Gerald and Dori Vance, and Dave Scott for use of photos and to the Quesnel Museum in British Columbia for special access to the haunted doll, Mandy.

Thanks to the editing finesse of Dale Triplett and the excellent graphics work of Eddie at SMAK Graphics.

I'm sure there are many others who should get a shout out, so please don't take any omissions personally, rather, consider this a blanket statement of gratitude to anyone I may have inadvertently overlooked.

Introduction

"In the same way as birds make a nest of anything, children make a doll of no matter what." –Victor Hugo.

For hundreds of years children have played with dolls. They are universal. They have been a part of the human experience for thousands of years. Where children are found, so are dolls. In the narrow sense, dolls can be defined as a representation of a human figure to be played with as a toy by a child. But there's much more to dolls than this simple definition.

In 2004, a stone doll was unearthed at an archeological dig on the Mediterranean island of Pantelleria. Dating of the doll revealed it to be 4,000 years old. Another doll was found at an archeological dig in Siberia, dated around 4,500 years old. The British Museum has examples of ancient Egyptian rag dolls made of papyrus-stuffed linen. In fact, hundreds of examples of antique dolls have been unearthed over the decades. They are made from rags, cloth, sticks and stone, porcelain and vinyl, rubber, metal and more.

But they are not always strictly toys. Dolls have long had an instructional function in many cultures. From reinforcing social norms and behaviors, to teaching cultural lore and traditions.

As Patricia Hogan, curator of The Strong National Museum of Play in Rochester, New York states:

"I think there is quite a tradition of using dolls to reflect cultural values and how we see children or who we wish them to be."

Strong, who is also the editor of the *American Journal of Play*, describes how, by the end of the 19th century, many parents stopped perceiving their children as unfinished adults and started looking at childhood as a time of innocence that needed to be protected. As a result dolls changed and became softer in appearance.

It was during this same period the manufacturing of toys became widespread and competing doll-makers began to create more realistic dolls. A larger range of materials became available, various mechanisms were utilized, and suddenly there were ranges of dolls that could exhibit more human-like qualities.

More mass-produced dolls meant more attention towards them in general. In 1816, German writer E.T.A. Hoffman published *"The Sandman,"* a story credited as the first tale in the "creepy doll genre." It was one of the turning points in the perception, on a larger scale, of dolls and their potential creepy factor.

Once the world of entertainment had its hooks into the idea of dolls as a useful component in horror stories, a range of creepy, even homicidal dolls made their way into the mainstream. Movies and television have made wide use of this theme, from the Twilight Zone's Talky Tina, to Chucky from the Child's Play franchise.

Movie characters are one thing, but most people leave such horrors behind when they exit the theatre, why then do so many people find dolls disturbing?

Dolls can of course be perceived in many ways and, just as they can be made FROM anything, they can be made INTO anything; from comforting companions to vessels for the demonic. And entertainment-related dolls aside, there's another idea that has long been connected to the world of dolls—the concept that they can be vessels for a wide range of otherworldly entities: from the lost, wandering spirits of children, to nasty, demonic entities that use dolls as a way to lure in the innocent.

Some of these feelings towards dolls may be due to the fact that many cultures have utilized human-like figures in magic rituals. From the legendary Voodoo doll, to European poppets, ancient examples demonstrate the use of dolls to curse and harm. In these cases, a doll is created to represent a specific person, and then ritually harmed to direct negative energy towards the person represented. These ritual and magical practices are one of the things that could instill energy, or a "presence" into a doll.

In modern times, as the paranormal has become more of a part of pop culture, interest in ghost hunting and haunted locations and/or objects has risen dramatically. In the midst of this interest, a small sub-culture has sprung up, one filled with those who collect haunted objects, and especially dolls.

There's an old precedent for haunted dolls. The 'granddaddy' of them is Robert, now kept in the East Martello museum in Key West, Florida. Robert's story goes back to the early 1900's, and he has been noted as an influence on modern haunted doll tales.

In the 1970's paranormal investigators Ed and Lorraine Warren took on a case that involved a haunted Raggedy Ann doll named Annabelle. She too is now famous, due in part to her appearance in recent horror movies.

But Robert and Annabelle are far from being alone, there are in fact hundreds of reportedly haunted dolls to be found around the world.

UK-based paranormal investigator Jayne Harris, well known for her previous association with Peggy the haunted doll, is also an online dealer in haunted objects. Asked in an interview why she believes so many dolls become haunted, she responded:

"Most of the time, the reason a doll becomes haunted is because of unfinished business. It could also be fear of passing-over, or sometimes there's somebody on the other side that the spirits don't want to reconnect with."

With so many dolls having reported paranormal activity, it would be almost impossible to chronicle them all. New ones are appearing, or being "discovered" on a regular basis.

I have of course covered the main, well known dolls that have a history of paranormal activity. Robert and Annabelle are here, but there are others that have gained some attention and snagged part of the spotlight in recent years. Peggy, Mandy and their kin are making waves in the study of haunted objects, and I've also dug up some other, lesser known stories I hope readers will find fascinating.

Examined too is the use of dolls in magic and rituals, paranormal locations that house haunted dolls, and of course, creepy dolls in entertainment.

With the success of films like Annabelle, and the continued popularity of online sales sites that deal in haunted dolls, there's likely much, much more to come in the field of such spooky objects.

Even people who don't have a defined fear of dolls, often have nervous reactions when confronted with certain figures. However much we believe a doll is not a likely threat, its human face creates a confusing and unsettling set of signals that strike at the core of our innate warning systems. Let's see if we can find out why.

I hope you enjoy this journey through the world of haunted dolls.

- David Weatherly

A Brief History of Dolls

It's difficult to trace the exact beginning of dolls. Historical examples have been discovered all over the world, demonstrating their universal development; however, the difficulty often lies in the blurry lines of use for the items. While some early examples have been clearly identified as items designed for play, others are more difficult to trace to their original use. Besides their use as toys, dolls have been used as ceremonial items, magical and ritual figures, healing proxies, and teaching tools. Just as dolls have many uses, they have been crafted from almost every material imaginable.

According to Robert Altman, expert on primitive arts and cultures:

"It is not always apparent whether a given sculptured effigy ought to be classified as puppet or doll, as component of a mask or simply as a statuette. Its function might be unknown, like that of the articulated clay figurines from prehistoric Mexico; or it might have multiple functions such as certain statuettes which were manipulated as sacred instruments of divination in several parts of the world, including ancient Egypt."

In *"The Doll,"* writers Fox and Landshoff further note:

"Long before their recorded history began, dolls were shaped from cloth, bone, stone, and clay. The museums of the world have in their collections a fascinating range of Neolithic images of female figures whose use can only be conjectured. They are catalogued as idols. We flatter ourselves in believing that progress is equated with modern man, and that these crude, often abstract shapes were made by childlike people whose entire waking and sleeping lives were spent in fear of the unknown. If they were childlike, then these primitive people must have spent some less fearful moments playing with their simply formed toys and dolls. Then, as now, the preponderant doll shape was female, and the male doll a rarity."

Some of the earliest figures which can be distinguished as dolls

1

were produced by the Egyptians and date from around 2000 B.C. These simple dolls were made from wood, and cut into a simple paddle shape. The shape of this type of doll lead to the common term, "paddle dolls" to denote this type of toy.

In the ancient world, dolls were often dedicated at temples to mark a life passage, such as the transition from childhood to puberty or marriage. Such special, ceremonial uses have ensured the survival of dolls in shrines.

A girl's doll might be dedicated to Aphrodite, the goddess of love, or Hera, the protector of marriage. In her youth, the poetess Sappho dedicated her doll to Aphrodite, later recording the incident:

"O Aphrodite, despise not my doll's little purple neckerchief. I, Sappho, dedicate this precious gift to you."

The Romans used bone, lead and terracotta to make dolls. An example of a Roman doll carved from oak was found in a tomb from the second century B.C. The doll is impressive, especially for the period during which it was created. It's articulated with mortice and tenon joints at the shoulders, thigh and even elbow. The artist who created the doll strived for a high degree of realism and the figure even has a well carved hairstyle to round out the human resemblance. The relic marks an important stage in the development of the basic shape of dolls.

Dolls carried great importance during the Roman empire. At the annual Saturnalia festival, dolls dedicated to the Gods were given to girls at puberty. If a young girl passed away, dolls might be offered to the gods of the underworld to help insure the child's peaceful transition to the world beyond, and perhaps give her companionship on the journey. In a young girl's tomb from the first century B.C., archeologists found her dolls along with items to adorn them, including cosmetics.

Oddly, one country that has very little historical record of children playing with dolls is China. There are few genuine, antique Chinese dolls that have been recovered, but there is evidence of dolls having magical significance. Widespread magical use may have led to the perception they were ritual items as opposed to playthings.

Other parts of Asia have strong traditions involving dolls. In Japan, the Doll Festival, also known as The Festival of the Peach Blossom, is held on the third day of the third month. Traditionally, it's a time for parents to pray for the protection of their children. Girls are given new kimonos and hair ribbons, and a ceremony is held during which the children entertain friends and family with food served on miniature, doll dishes.

Poor families construct dolls from paper for the festival, but among wealthy families, elaborate dolls and accessories are prominent. Some families add new dolls each year until the girl is grown and married. Many families start purchasing dolls from the time a girl is born, building the collection with each passing year. Eventually the ceremonial dolls are taken with the girl as part of her dowry. Some families have sets dating back several hundred years. The festival itself is said to be a continuous tradition that dates back to 70 B.C.

Dolls traditionally have special significance in India too, particularly during the Gokulashtami festival, the celebration of the birth of Krishna, the child god. The festival itself is primarily a children's festival, and a toy cradle holding a representation of Krishna is a feature of the celebration. Songs are sung over the figure, sweets and gifts are presented to children and dolls are one of the main items given.

In years past, Indian girls celebrated their own Gudiya festival during which the "Doll Wedding" was celebrated. It has fallen out of popularity in more modern times.

Throughout history, cultures have often used dolls as teaching tools and instructional figures to illustrate myths and cultural tales. In Ancient Greece, India and Japan, these instructions could impart important traditions involving the concepts of bravery and warrior traditions to boys, and cultural knowledge to girls. In cultures that transmitted their teachings and history primarily through oral traditions, dolls were powerful visual aids to further instill the information being relayed.

Often these teachings would blend spiritual traditions with the toy. For instance, in India, a woman might make an image of a household deity, and, while crafting it, explain the story of the deity to the children gathered around her. When the doll is passed on to the children, it has added significance, since they understand the background and mythical and spiritual story associated with the image.

Dolls were utilized in conjunction with other aspects of society too. They became a popular item at the royal courts of Europe, where they were used to exhibit fashion trends. In 1321, the queen of France sent a doll dressed in the latest fashions of France as a gift to the queen of England, wife of Edward II. The doll caused a sensation at the English court and benefited French dressmakers for years to follow.

Constance Eileen King, writing in the *Collector's History of Dolls*, emphasised that dolls cannot be dismissed lightly. She states:

"I have frequently purchased dolls from families who have kept the toy of a sister (or child who died in infancy), for sixty or seventy years, as the glass eyes of the small object, perhaps of wax and cloth, exerted its personality upon them to such affect that they could not bring themselves to discard it casually, but searched for a collector who would care for the item and relieve them of its presence. Though it is easy for the sophisticated to dismiss an object as 'just a doll,' one can begin to understand how a witchcraft representation can affect such awe, when a commercially-made, mass-produced china doll can force a sharp-tongued old bachelor to carry it shamefacedly in the bottom of a suitcase from one flat to another, because it once belonged to a sister who had died before he was born."

Wooden dolls were very popular in the late 1700's and early 1800's, and by the 1850's, dolls were being made with wax in much of Europe.

It was the 1800's that brought the first wave of significant changes in the world of dolls. Craftsmen in France found themselves in heated competition. As the top doll makers tried to one up each other, variations began to be produced that could mimic human qualities. As Fox and Landshoff note regarding the competing companies:

"...the zeal with which they obtained patents for new mechanical improvements—a crying doll, an eating doll, a double-faced doll, a nursing doll, a doll's head that could move in all directions, movable eyes and eyelids, a musical doll, a breathing doll whose chest could simulate rhythmic inhaling and exhaling, as well as dolls that walked, talked, and threw a kiss."

In the 1860's doll-makers in France and Germany began creating dolls with metal parts. Heads, hands and legs were being made from a variety of materials including copper, lead, brass, zinc, tin, pewter and aluminum. By the 1870's, American companies also filed patents on metal dolls.

Another dramatic change in the doll industry came in 1889. In Ithaca, New York, Celia and Charity Smith started drawing dolls on cotton and selling them by the yard. The dolls could be cut out and stuffed by mothers and children. The pre-drawn dolls were cheap and popular. Their huge success spawned numerous imitations. The do-it-yourself dolls led to the development of manufactured rag dolls whose faces were stiffened with muslin.

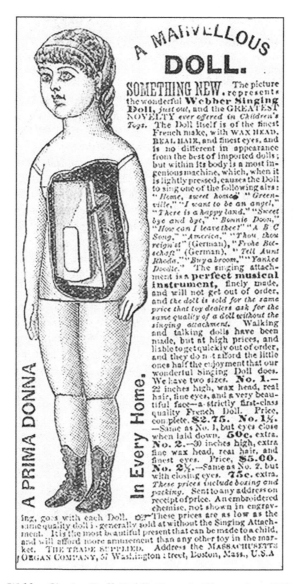

Webber Singing Doll. Public Domain illustration, 1882.

Ultimately the world of dolls changed dramatically with large scale manufacturing. The development of commercial markets led to greater numbers of dolls around the world. Additionally, the widespread concept of dolls as primarily a toy for children, girls in particular, rose, and the use of dolls as ritual items declined. Declined, but did not die.

We shall look further at the magical connections to dolls through history and into modern times, and how this may be an aspect of modern, haunted dolls.

To children, as well as adults, dolls can represent a wide range of emotional and personal significance. As Fox and Landshoff state:

"To the child, the doll is a presence. It is forever on the threshold of becoming, of being — of being whatever the child or adult breathes into it. His utterances may be gibberish or cabalistic, and beyond the boundaries frozen by traditional concepts of meaning. The doll is a private vessel into which are distilled fears, hopes, sorrows, and make-believe. The diabolical is not less than the angelic. One begins with innocence, and the experience of time may be as secret as the confessional or as brash as theatricals to an audience coaxed with ice cream and cookies. Nothing and everything is revealed, the heart laid bare. 'To this crib I always took my doll; human beings must love something, and in the dearth of worthier objects of affection, I contrived to find a pleasure in loving and cherishing a faded graven image, shabby as a miniature scarecrow. It puzzles me now to remember with what absurd sincerity I doted on this little toy, half fancying it alive and capable of sensation. I could not sleep unless it was folded in my night-gown; and when it lay there safe and warm, I was comparatively happy, believing it to by happy likewise.'"

A Brief History of Dolls

Creepy Little Things_

San Clemente, California 2014. Families in the suburban Talega neighborhood started finding porcelain dolls on their doorsteps. A total of ten dolls were discovered by eight different families, causing concern to many residents. As if the mysterious manifestation of the dolls wasn't creepy enough, the porcelain figures were made in the likeness of little girls living in the homes where they were left. Distraught parents feared someone was stalking their daughters.

The Orange County Sheriff's Department was contacted, and deputies arrived to investigate the situation involving the eerie dolls. Initially, officials weren't sure whether the dolls were intended as a prank, or whether something more sinister was unfolding. According to Lt. Jeff Hallock:

"People are saying the dolls slightly resemble their daughters, which is creepy. There doesn't appear to be an obvious pattern to who has been targeted either. We're examining the dolls in an attempt to identify who may have manufactured them. We don't know if it's a prank, we don't know if particular families were specifically motivated or targeted."

Newscaster Brittney Hopper with KCAL9 interviewed one of the mothers who found a doll on her family's doorstep:

"We're very unsettled and obviously taking this very seriously as it concerns our daughters and little girls."

Other members of the community expressed concerns too. One woman said her daughter was quite upset at receiving the doll. Even neighbors who didn't receive one of the unwanted gifts were concerned:

"It leaves an impression on your kid. Can you imagine your daughter getting that? It would freak me out too."

Another mother echoed similar thoughts:

"We're a little concerned. It's creepy!"

Fortunately, the mystery was solved in short order. Officers tracked down the source of the dolls—a woman from the local church the families attended. The woman thought leaving the dolls would be a kind gesture of friendship and that the little girls would enjoy the toys. Authorities told reporters:

"Investigators have concluded that [the neighbor's] motivation was out of goodwill and that she intended it as a kind gesture. There will be no further investigation of this case."

While the San Clemente dolls proved to be a situation with completely innocent motivations, it's interesting to note the strong reactions of the families and community to the appearance of what they quickly dubbed "creepy dolls."

The fear of dolls is called "Pediophobia" and is relatively common. In technical terms, pediophobia translates as "fear of little children." It's linguistically close to "pedophobia" the fear of actual living children. Pediophobia is a branch of the larger tree of automatonophobia, or, the fear of humanoid figures. This includes not just dolls, but dummies, mannequins, wax figures, robots and even statues. Some people are afraid of all dolls and stuffed toys, others fear a specific type. Dolls that talk or move, and dolls that are old fashioned are often noted as especially frightening.

Pediophobia is usually rooted in a disturbing childhood experience. Those suffering from the phobia may have had a frightening incident involving a doll or similar toy, or, they may have suffered dreams or nightmares about dolls doing things normally impossible.

As with many phobias, the actual event may have been forgotten by the conscious mind, but the subconscious holds on to the information and attempts to keep the person from putting themselves in danger, using the identifiers (the fear) as one of the markers of danger. The individual suffering from such a phobia is likely well aware the fear is irrational, yet they are powerless to do anything about it. Fear, any fear, is a difficult thing to conquer.

In practical terms, the fear of dolls can create symptoms that include: anxiety, feelings of dread, nausea, heart palpitations, uncontrollable shaking, and difficulty breathing. One sufferer, who prefers to remain anonymous, attempts to convey his feelings when confronted with dolls, citing a particular incident from his own experience:

"I can't make people understand the fear. I know it sounds silly, but I'm terrified, absolutely terrified, of dolls. All kinds of dolls. I was working on a job where I had to make house calls. I ended up in a room alone at this house. I was doing my work and suddenly I just had this weird feeling. I turned around, and there it was, there was this damn doll sitting up on a shelf across the room. It had a shiny porcelain head and big, dark eyes. I felt like it was staring at me, like it had been the whole time. I lost it. I could not stay in that home. I rushed out of the door in a sheer panic. People don't understand the intensity of this kind of fear unless they suffer from it, I just can't make people understand the degree of fear I experience, if I have to deal with a doll like that in that kind of situation. Little girl's rooms are the worst, I had to quit that job."

People suffering from uncontrollable pediophobia will go out of their way to avoid situations that lead to them having to deal with dolls and associated figures. This often means avoiding friends or family's homes that have dolls, and even stores that sell dolls.

The fear has even been known to manifest in children, causing them to exhibit similar symptoms to adults who suffer.

"I blame Chucky!" Declares Becca Hisle, a porcelain dollmaker from Texas.

Hisle believes movies like the Child's Play series have instilled an irrational fear of dolls in people. She has been involved with doll-making for over thirty years, and says it's the realistic aspects of dolls, especially porcelain ones, her specialty, that put people off:

"They look real. People get spooked because they don't like the eyes, and they're too lifelike. The black eyes do look real. I don't find them spooky at all, to me, it's a lot of fun."

While Hisle uses the word "spooky," the most common term people seem to use when describing their uneasy feelings around dolls is "creepy."

The term "creepy" in the modern sense of the word, has been around since the middle of the 19th century when it appeared in a news article about a ghost in *The New York Times* in 1877. Since then, it has been applied to a wide range of items and ideas and it's now often heard in conjunction with dolls, mostly because of their lifelike qualities.

Historians state these qualities appeared when craftsmen and manufacturers figured out how to utilize materials that created more lifelike looking dolls. In the early 1900s, more mechanisms began to be utilized that added to the human-like aspects in the figures. The "sleep eye" mechanism for instance, causes a doll to close its eyes for sleep when laid in a horizontal position. Over the decades, variations of lifelike qualities have been utilized in doll production.

Beyond the phobia and its drive to keep people "safe" from the threat of dolls, the sense that dolls are "creepy" may have even deeper cultural implications.

In 2013, Frank McAndrew, a psychologist at Knox College in Illinois, and Sara Koehnke, a graduate student, published a paper on their working hypothesis about what "creepiness" means. The paper was based on the results of a survey of more than 1,300 people to learn what "creeped" them out. It's interesting to note that collecting dolls was named as one of the "creepiest" hobbies.

The pair's study on creepiness had some additional findings, including the perception that most "creepy people" don't realize they're perceived as being creepy by others. Those who believe that hobbies like doll collecting have a creep factor have strong feelings on the matter, and the emotions evoked may be deeply seated. As the study reports:

"We're creeped out by people who have these kinds of hobbies and occupations because, right away, we jump to the conclusion, 'What kind of person would willingly surround themselves with...humanlike things that are not human?' We're on guard to those types of people because they're out of the ordinary."

In part, it's the fact that many people perceive the hobby of collecting dolls as something beyond the acceptable social norm. As McAndrew states, creepiness comes down to uncertainty:

"You're getting mixed messages. If something is clearly frightening, you scream, you run away. If something is disgusting, you know how to act. But if something is creepy...it might be dangerous but you're not sure it is... there's an ambivalence.

If someone is acting outside of accepted social norms—standing too close, or staring, say—we become suspicious of their intentions. But in absence of real evidence of a threat, we wait, and in the meantime, call them creepy. The upshot, is that being in a state of 'creeped out' makes you 'hyper-vigilant.'"

It's interesting that McAndrew uses the example of someone staring. Many people who suffer from fear of dolls, note one of the things they find most unsettling about dolls is the fact that they "stare" and their eyes appear to follow you around the room. The study's point about hyper-vigilance and the ways in which humans process potential threats is interesting too. Dolls, when perceived as creepy, present a confusing challenge for the brain to process. There is no clear or obvious threat, yet the human-like components displayed by a doll cause many people's alarm bells to go off. Since dolls are made to look "human," the mind attempts to connect as it would with another human, looking for emotional indications, facial movements and other body language. None of which a normal, inanimate doll will manifest.

Since the very survival of the human race has long been dependent on avoided threats and dangerous situations, the creepiness factor may well be one of the primary forces that has allowed the species to survive long term. A manifestation of the sixth sense applied to unusual situations.

Delving further into the idea of creepiness, McAndrews continues:

"From an evolutionary perspective, people who responded with this creeped-out response did better in the long run. People who didn't might have ignored dangerous things, or they're more likely to jump to the wrong conclusion too quickly and be socially ostracized.

It really focuses your attention and helps you process any relevant information to help you decide whether there is something to be afraid of or not. I really think creepiness is where we respond in situations where we don't know enough or have enough information to respond, but we have enough to put us on our guard."

Modern pop culture has also played a role in the perception of dolls as creepy. The wide-ranging perception has been heightened by popular entertainment, and movie makers have exploited the creepy factor associated with dolls to make box office blockbusters. But there's certainly a precedent for the effective use of dolls to scare.

Why do so many people find dolls disturbing? Photo by author.

Older generations will surely remember "Talky Tina," the living doll that terrorized Telly Savalas in a classic episode of the Twilight Zone. Not long after, the film "Magic" hit movie screens with its depiction of a living ventriloquist dummy. More recent additions to this sub-genre of horror include the Chucky series and the current Annabelle movies.

But the creepiness of dolls hasn't done anything to hurt sales figures; in fact, some people believe it even helped bolster it since a number of offshoots of the market have developed, centered around haunted and creepy dolls.

Annual sales of dolls make up a major portion of toy sales each year. In 2011, doll sales reached $2.66 billion dollars in the US alone. By 2014, the figure had declined to $2.32 billion. Even today, doll sales still outpace sales of plush toys, arts and crafts toys and a range of other playthings. In fact, when it comes to toys, doll sales come in second only to sports and outdoor toys.

None of these figures count the bustling secondhand market of antique and collectible dolls, some of which garner prices in the thousands or even tens of thousands of dollars.

In September 2014, a rare doll made by Kämmer & Reinhardt in the 1900s went up for auction and sold for the unbelievable price of $395,750. No word on whether or not the doll is haunted.

Haunted dolls themselves have become a market of their own with a bustling trade taking place, often on auction sites like eBay.

Haunted dolls have often made the news in recent years. Even NPR (National Public Radio) chimed in on the topic with a story titled "Haunted Dolls are a Thing." The broadcast highlighted Robert the Doll, the iconic antique that once belonged to Key West artist Eugene Otto. Robert now "lives" at the East Martello Museum in Florida and is a popular attraction for tourists, ghost hunters, and curiosity seekers.

Even non-haunted, "creepy" dolls have their own market and have become very popular. A prime example is the now well-known "Living Dead Dolls." A series of figures made intentionally creepy, in the image of iconic supernatural characters like vampires and zombies. New releases in the Living Dead Dolls line quickly sell out and become collector's items, with many going for high prices in the aftermarket. The doll line appeals to both those interested in the supernatural as well as horror movie fans.

Director John Leonetti of the Conjuring franchise film "Annabelle," told the Huffington Post, dolls make exceptional vehicles for horror movies:

"If you think about them, most dolls are emulating a human figure, but they're missing one big thing, which is emotion. So they're shells. It's a natural psychological and justifiable vehicle for demons to take over. If you look at a doll in its eyes, it just stares. That's creepy. They're hollow inside. That space needs to be filled."

But some want to fill those shells themselves and seek out dolls that are as realistic as possible.

In 2004, A.F. Robertson launched an investigation into doll collecting and collectors. His study, titled "Life Like Dolls: The Collector Doll Phenomenon and the Lives of the Women Who Love Them," revealed some interesting findings. According to Robertson, some of the women studied thought of their dolls as living, sentient beings with feelings and emotions. These people referred to their collections as "nurseries." These collectors represent a subset of "normal" doll collectors, and are usually rejected by other collectors because of their "relationships" with their dolls.

Some women, such as the ones Robertson studied, treat their dolls as real babies. The dolls are called "reborns," a concept psychologist's refer to as "transition objects" for people dealing with loss, grief or anxiety. Reborns are hyper-realistic, custom crafted dolls made by artists that are marketed as dolls "you can love forever."

Many of these reborn dolls have heartbeats, breathing motions, and make cooing sounds just as a living baby would. These dolls are highly prized by those who desire them, but are perceived as being "extra creepy" by much of the general populace. Reborns are even unsettling for many "normal" doll collectors.

Such extreme realism in created objects leads us to another fascinating topic that comes up when addressing the perceptions and effects dolls have on people. Many experts believe lifelike dolls dwell firmly in the middle of a place called the "uncanny valley."

Rather than a physical place, the uncanny valley is actually an aesthetic examined by scientists and psychologists that deals with the relationship between the degree of an object's resemblance to a human being and a living person's emotional response to such an object.

The recent version of the concept dates back to 1970 and Japanese robotics professor Masahiro Mori. It was translated and further defined by author Jasia Reichardt in his 1978 book "Robots: Fact, Fiction and Prediction." But the concept appears to have originated with an essay by Ernst Jentsch, "On the Psychology of the Uncanny" in 1906, and was further elaborated on by Sigmund Freud in a 1919 essay titled "The Uncanny." Freud discussed the idea that the uncanny recalled repressed fears and anti-social desires and that discomfort was rooted in uncertainty. The uncertainty perhaps, of the perception of things not quite human even though they appear human.

Mori, the scientist who studied the topic in the 1970s, found that when a robot became more human, the observer's emotional responses to the artificial construct became increasingly positive and empathetic until it reached a point beyond where the response quickly turned to strong revulsion. This area, between something barely human, and something that appears fully human, is the uncanny valley.

Given this paradigm, it's clear some dolls firmly take their place of residence in the uncanny valley, dwelling in a zone where they create eerie and creepy feelings in many who observe or interact with them.

The uncanny valley is still a controversial subject of study. Some scholars disagree with the concept and believe the "uncanny valley" doesn't really exist, but others are convinced the notion of people being disturbed by inhuman objects that act human is quite valid. The entire field of study has become more complex in our modern age with large scale focus on constructed, artificial life.

It's true recent advancements in robotics and A.I. (artificial intelligence) have brought renewed attention to the concept of the uncanny valley, but the ideas inherent in the study can easily be applied to things beyond robots, and specifically for the purposes of this book, dolls.

On a base, human level, the principles of the uncanny valley suggest that objects which appear human, or almost human, elicit feelings of unease, revulsion and/or creepiness within observers, and dolls certainly fall into this paradigm.

Other studies have addressed the psychological aspects associated with objects that display human attributes but are not human.

A study published in 2012 in *Psychological Science* by researchers from the University of Groningen in the Netherlands, reached some interesting conclusions. The team found that inappropriate, nonverbal mimicry produced a physical response in observers that "creeped them out" and gave them chills.

Dolls don't mimic, but they do make "eye contact" and this confuses the human brain to a certain degree. When this eye contact occurs, warning signals are quickly sent to the brain and, since the doll is not human, the observer's brain has difficulty understanding what is transpiring and where the threat lies. It's illogical, but frightening nonetheless.

As McAndrew stated in his study:

"We shouldn't be afraid of a little piece of plastic, but it's sending out social signals. They look like people but aren't people, so we don't know how to respond to it, just like we don't know how to respond when we don't know whether there is a danger or not…the world in which we evolved how we process information, there weren't things like dolls."

The fact is, many people are actually drawn TO creepiness. The discomfort it creates is edgy, and while it's not enough to be terrifying, it is compelling. When a good storyteller steps in and takes something like Chucky or Talky Tina in hand, the dynamic is both powerful and disturbing at the same time.

"Creepy" dolls aren't going anywhere, and in fact, we can expect more and more in popular media. And as scientists continue to experiment with artificial life, we will see more life-sized constructs that closely mimic humans. A terrifying potential for those suffering automatonophobia.

Dolls & the World of Magic, Possessions & Hauntings

There are countless stories of haunted, possessed, and cursed dolls. So, what is it exactly that makes them prime targets for paranormal activity?

John Zaffis, veteran investigator and expert in haunted items, has an extensive collection of haunted objects gathered during his many years working in the field. His collection has more dolls with "paranormal problems" than any other type of object. Reflecting on why this may be the case, Zaffis says it's because dolls are among the best vessels for supernatural activity:

"Dolls are among the best targets for spirit activity. They are like miniature people, and when children play with them, they animate the dolls and give them personalities with their imagination. Adults relate to them in the same way."

John makes an excellent point when he states that dolls are like "miniature people." This principle is one of the reasons dolls have been used extensively throughout history as focal points for magical rituals. More often than not with evil intent, but there are other uses too. In fact, cultures far and wide have long utilized dolls in various types of ritual magic. From prosperity and healing dolls, to poppets designed to hurt, maim and kill, to dolls used to forecast the future, there seems to be no limit to their magical use. These ideas aren't new at all and in fact can be found far back in history. As Richard Cavendish states in "Man, Myth and Magic:"

"The use of a doll, made of wax, clay, lead or other material, to kill, injure or seduce the person the doll represents, is known from Egypt and Mesopotamia, from India, Greece and Rome, and from all over the world, ancient and modern."

Historically, the most common type of doll used for magical purposes is a poppet. Specifically, the poppet is used in "sympathetic

19

magic" workings. Following the theory that "like creates like," the poppet is used as a focal point, a representation of the intended target. The magical principle is that, since the doll represents person X, then whatever is done to the doll will happen to person X. This connection is established by creating the doll in the victim's image. Adding personal items taken from the target to the doll, and carrying out designated ritual processes to further enhance the sympathetic connection empowers the ritual further.

Early examples of such magical effigies were used by European, Native American, and African cultures. The European poppet has roots among the Germanic and Scandinavian tribes who used them for ceremonial purposes. This practice is still alive in modern times by Wiccans, Voodoo practitioners, and others who have adapted the principle to their own magical ceremonial workings.

Historic Ritual Dolls

In Ancient Egypt, enemies of Rameses III attempted to bring about his death using wax images made in his likeness. Dolls had long been used for magical purposes in Egypt and it was believed the images themselves took on a living energy. Anything done to the doll would in turn cause the same effect on the person it was made to represent because the doll was alive. Egyptian magicians also used ritual dolls for positive goals, often to remove sickness or evil from the body of a living person.

The Romans and the Greeks both utilized dolls in rituals, in some cases, as a way to connect with the gods, in others, as sympathetic magic especially for purposes of love and war.

One of the leading authorities on Greek magic, Professor Christopher Faraone, of the University of Chicago, says the ancient Greeks sometimes used poppets, or "kolossoi," as they called them, to restrain spirits and dangerous entities. On other occasions, the images were used in an attempt to bind lovers together. Faraone notes an account written about 200 B.C.E., wherein the tragedian Theocritus refers to melting and burning wax dolls, and the tale of Simaetha, rejected by Delphis, who attempts to get her lover back using black magic on wax images.

In Heian period Japan (794-1185), dolls were made of paper and grass on certain days of the year. The dolls were then rubbed over an individual's body as a way of exorcising physical misfortunes and negative energies.

Another version of such charms, called "Somin-Shorai," were made of wood and had six faces. Each side of the doll was inscribed with the words Somin-Shorai. The dolls were used to drive off evil spirits, clearing the way for luck and good fortune. They are still sold today at New Year's Day celebrations.

Around the same period, Buddhist priests were using dolls to illustrate their teachings. The dolls were helpful for lower classes that could neither read nor write, and hence needed a graphic representation to help them understand new spiritual teachings.

Yet another magical Japanese doll is called "Hoko-san." Hoko-san are usually made of papier-mâché, and measure from three to six inches. At night they are placed in the beds of sick children. The next morning, the doll is thrown into the sea. It's believed the doll is capable of pulling the sickness from a suffering child. Once the illness is instilled in the doll, throwing the effigy in the water takes the disease far away from the victim and they are healed.

In China, there's little record of children playing with dolls. Dolls were given great magical significance around the country, and as a result, were not deemed suitable as playthings. Such figures were often used to magically attack enemies. Typically, a straw doll would be used, dressed in blood-stained paper, and pierced with needles while reciting incantations.

A similar process was reputedly used in parts of Korea. Curiously, the word for doll in both the Chinese and Korean languages derives from the same root as the words for idol and fetish, another indication of the primarily magical origins of dolls in both cultures.

In terms of magical use, Europe has a rich history of doll magic. In fact, one famous case comes from Britain and involves dolls being used for death magic.

In England, in 1324, King Edward II was extremely unpopular. The discontented citizens wanted to keep their heads, so open rebellion wasn't an option. In search of a solution, a group in Coventry approached a notable local magician known as John of Nottingham. The group gave the sorcerer a list of targets and asked him to apply his necromantic skills to bring about the demise of those oppressing them. The king of course, was at the top of the list, but there were other key members of the royal court included as targets.

It was a big task to take on, but the magician was willing to attempt it. Nottingham and his assistant, Robert Marshall, collected seven pounds of wax and several yards of cloth, and proceeded to create effigies of the intended victims.

But before making a magical assassination run at the king, the magician wanted to test his skills and make sure he had the ritual down pat. Nottingham and Marshall chose a control subject—Richard de Lowe, a local man without any particular political leaning. As was later recorded, de Lowe *"Somewhat inconsiderately was included for experimental purposes."*

The two magical workers took up residence in an old ruined house and proceeded with their undertaking. The process took several days. Finally, on a Friday at the stroke of midnight, *"a curious pin wrought of sharp lead"* was driven two inches deep into the forehead of the figure representing de Lowe.

The following day, Nottingham sent a servant to de Lowe's home to check on the man's condition. The servant found de Lowe in a miserable state. Crying and screaming like a madman, de Lowe had lost his memory and was disorientated, unable to recognize anyone or anything around him. He remained in the same state until dawn on Sunday, at which point the magician removed the pin from the doll's head and thrust it into the image's heart. A few days later, Richard de Lowe died.

Now confident in the accuracy of his magic, Nottingham prepared to utilize the same process to go after the King and his royal associates, all for a fee, of course.

The sorcerer didn't have a chance to act however. His assistant Robert Marshall had become nervous at the prospect of attacking the king in any form, and went to the authorities, reporting on Nottingham and those who had employed him. The magician was ratted out by his own assistant.

Nottingham was arrested, and despite his run to the authorities, Robert Marshall along with him. Twenty-seven other conspirators were rounded up and they all stood trial, along with the magician and his cohort. All twenty-nine pled not guilty and by the time the proceedings were done, they were all acquitted. Nottingham himself died in prison while awaiting the trial's conclusion.

John of Nottingham's trial marks one of the earliest recorded incidents of a case brought against a magician for attempted murder using ritual magic, but it wouldn't be the last, especially once church authorities got involved in the pursuit of witches and practitioners of black magic.

As noted in "Man, Myth & Magic," there were accounts during witch trials of dolls or images being used for magical purposes:

"The quickest way to murder someone by witchcraft, according to old Mother Demdike at the trial of the Lancashire witches in 1612 is to 'make a Picture of clay, like unto the shape of the person whom they mean to kill, and dry it thoroughly: and when they would have them to be ill in any one place more than another; then take a Thorn or a Pin, and prick it in that part of the Picture you would so have to be ill: and when you would have any part of the body to consume away, then take that part of the Picture, and burn it. And when they would have the whole body to consume away, then take the remnant of said Picture and burn it: and so thereupon by that means, the body shall die.'"

Other examples of such statements came out as the witch trials raged across Europe. Years after the Lancashire trial, a pair of sorcerers were put on trial for magical workings with a clay figure. In 1649, John Palmer and Elizabeth Knott made a clay figure of a woman they wanted to curse. In the course of their ritual, the pair put the magical figure on a fire. As it slowly roasted, the victim writhed in agony. When the clay figure was completely consumed by the flames, the woman died. Palmer and Knott were put on trial and didn't fare as well as the sorcerer of Nottingham—they were found guilty and executed at St. Albans.

Africa too has its share of magical dolls. The "nkisi," or "bocio," are traditional effigy-like dolls from West and Central Africa. The dolls are used in specific rituals, usually in healing rites, or for protection, and on occasion, to bind evil spirits.

During the early days of the slave trade, Africans carried these concepts with them to the American colonies. To the Africans at the time, the images were a magical fetish, something carried as a talisman for protection or power. The items were feared by slave owners since they were a potential sign of witchcraft and dark, unknown powers. Slaves caught carrying a fetish were often put to death. It was only later in the slave trade period, when African and European magical traditions blended together, that slaves began using dolls as focal points for curses.

Other African cultures made use of dolls too. The Yoruba culture believes the souls of twins are indivisible. When the death of a twin occurs, the mother of the surviving twin forever carries an image of the dead child. The mother bathes and dresses the image at the same time as she does her living child, and the spirit twin is given a place to live with the family. The doll in this case embodies the deceased's spirit.

According to Malcolm Gaskill in "Witchcraft and Evidence in Early Modern England," a member of the royal family practiced sympathetic magic on dolls due to her unhappy marriage:

Caroline of Brunswick, the one-time Princess of Wales, was married to the man who later became King George IV. The Princess couldn't stand the man, and she spent many hours creating wax dolls of him which she jabbed viciously with pins.

The account of Caroline's magical workings was verified by Lady Charlotte Campbell in her diary for 1814. She records that the wife of the then Prince Regent frequently made the images with ill intent and tortured them:

"One evening after dinner, she made one of these dolls and gave it an amiable addition of large horns; then took three pins out of her garment and stuck them through, and put the figure to roast and melt on the fire."

There's no record of exactly what effect the practice had on her husband, if any, however, when Caroline finally ran off to Italy with her young lover, George didn't protest. The royal pair remained married but lived separately until Caroline's death in 1821.

Another doll curiosity that became popular in the 1800's were fortune telling dolls. Fortune telling dolls were desired, trendy, conversation pieces during the period. They were lightweight, wooden figures, easy to take to parties. Pastel colored sheets were cut into an attractive, scalloped design, threaded together around the narrow end, and attached to the waist of the doll to represent the full skirt of the figure's dress.

The upper classes enjoyed the figures and even Princess Victoria had a fortune telling doll in her collection. It gave advice such as "Happy and blest with the man you love best" and "You'll have a boy to bring you joy."

In Germany, craftsman B. Voight patented an "Oracle Doll" in 1891. Though it's sought after by collectors, there don't seem to be any surviving examples or any clear indication of how the doll worked.

As the century turned, despite "modern and rational thought," the use of dolls as magical proxies didn't fade away. In 1900, a figure of United States President McKinley was found on the steps of the American Embassy in London. The figure was riddled with pins and burned. The intent was clear.

While pins are the most common method to inflict harm on dolls, and by default the intended victim, dolls can also be burned, broken, mangled and twisted. They can be hung from trees, or suspended in a chimney to slowly suffer from smoke inhalation. Other methods include slowly roasting a doll over flames, dunking it in boiling water, or throwing it in running water so that the movement of the water wears the doll, and the target, down.

Likewise, there are numerous processes to "charge" dolls and connect them to the person they are intended to represent.

According to Bernard Bromage writing in "The Occult Arts of Ancient Egypt:"

"An image can be charged in a number of ways: inverted 'prayer,' the burning of incense; actual blood sacrifice in its vicinity; the sheer impact of petrifying venom—all these can play their part in causing an image—especially one already associated with destruction—to spring into a black, abounding vitality which can burn itself into the conscious and subconscious, especially during sleep."

Infamous magician Aleister Crowley mentions this form of sympathetic magic in his novel "Moonchild." Crowley emphasizes the importance of linking the doll with the victim, as a focal point of the magician's hatred towards his intended target:

"It is not enough to pretend that your wax image is the person you want to bewitch, you must make a real connection. That is the whole art of magic, to be able to do that."

Crowley, like many magicians of his time, had studied classical lore and magical texts and was familiar with the already established process of sympathetic magic. As Sir James George Frazer notes in the classic, "The Golden Bough," sympathetic magic, or mimicry is one of the two basic principles of magic and is effective because:

> *"…like produces like, or that an effect resembles its cause."*

Frazer calls the other basic magic principle "the law of contact or contagion," essentially:

> *"…that things which have once been in contact with each other continue to act on each other at a distance after the physical contact has been severed."*

These two ritual principles are often combined in practice, especially when it comes to sympathetic magic. A doll, as the representative figure, is further empowered by adding something that has been in contact with the intended target; hair, nail clippings, clothing, etc. The figure can then be utilized with the belief that *"…things act on each other at a distance through a secret sympathy."*

It is, in principle, a simple belief. The image of the victim IS the victim. While the idea may sound ridiculous to those of some religious faiths, magical practitioners like to note that such a widespread belief has taken many forms throughout the years. After all, Catholics believe relics that once belonged to saints carry their blessed energy, and can in turn bestow blessing on individuals who come in contact with the item. It's one example of another form of sympathetic magic, the idea that one thing represents another, and through the energetic connection, results can be achieved.

While history is full of cases involving ritual dolls, modern eras have seen their fair share. Fast forwarding to 1964, the figure of a naked woman, six inches long and made from modeling clay was found in Sandringham in Norfolk. The figure was pierced with a piece of silver hawthorn through its heart. It's not known whether the magic done on the figure was intended to cause harm, or perhaps someone was trying to pierce the target's heart with love, essentially making the victim have "heartache" for the person casting the spell.

Another case received media attention in the 1970's.

England, Halloween night, 1976:

Householders living near a small patch of woods known as "The Scrubs," were disturbed by piercing screams. Approaching the woods as closely as they could, the witnesses saw fires burning among the trees. Exercising caution, the witnesses withdrew from the scene and waited until daylight to investigate further.

The next day, they found clear evidence of what they described as "a black magic ceremony." In the clearing amid the trees was a twenty-foot diameter circle of logs, painted white, likely so that it could be seen in the darkness. In the center of the circle lay what was described by the press as "The Doll of Death."

The doll itself was a clay figure made to represent a man. It was painted red to simulate blood, and it was clearly the focal point of the previous night's rituals. Nails had been used to pierce the figure and the phallus was mutilated. The surrounding trees were decorated with black magic symbols, and the earth in the circle bore a pentacle around which, strangely, were hoof marks.

No further information surfaced about the case and it's likely the people who held the ceremony simply went about their business and kept their mouths shut. The press loved the situation, after all, the event happened in "witch country," and such topics made good headlines in the 1970's.

Over the years, I have at times consulted with police departments on matters involving so called "occult crimes." It's amazing how frequently ritual dolls are found at sites where ceremonies have taken place. Frequently, these sites are clearly left by what I would term "non-trained" magical practitioners attempting to gain something using magic. Teenagers are often the culprits at sites where "satanic" markings are found. Black, inverted pentagrams, items stolen from graveyards, and animal sacrifice are ways rebellious youth think they can cast a spell to achieve their goals. These cases have gotten worse over the years with the advent of the Internet and the numerous do it yourself magical "spell books" commonly available online.

The dolls in these cases are usually used to get revenge on someone, a scorned focus of affection, a teacher or authority figure, or even a parent. At times, the victim's name is even found on the dolls.

But frankly, these cases are the ones that are less concerning. Other incidents involve people who are trained in magical traditions, utilizing dolls in very careful ritual undertakings to hit their target with a range of effects, from minor illnesses, to more dire troubles. As W.G. Gray notes in "Magical Ritual Methods," there's a component to such magic that, when refined, is quite powerful. The trick of course, is in the proper procedure and direct, intentional focus:

"In more sophisticated magical theory what harms the victim is the concentrated malice of the sorcerer, for which the image acts as a focus. In

the making of the doll, in the gleeful torture of it, the magician arouses his own inner hatred, concentrates it and projects it at his enemy. If the image is accidentally damaged, the victim is not harmed. Only when the image is 'charged' with hatred and deliberately maltreated does the victim feel the effects. The rites of 'charging' are ways of concentrating the sorcerer's fury but, even so, the image takes on an evil vitality of its own."

Gray's book is fascinating and offers other insights, not only on how powerful the ritual process can be, but also the psychological aspects that aid in the effectiveness of image magic:

"It is significant that the images are so often called dolls, 'child's babies,' poppets, puppets, or mommets—names which point to the roots of image magic in the experience of childhood. A child accepts that a doll is alive, is a person, and can be cosseted or hurt. For many sorcerers of the past, the fact that the doll represented the victim, and the mimic torments inflicted on it, would be enough by themselves to cause the victim harm."

It may be that the magical process itself often leads to dolls becoming "haunted" or "possessed." But it's not too big of a leap to begin to understand why so many seemingly normal dolls can become "haunted." As Father Gary Thomas, the exorcist portrayed in the film, "The Rite" notes:

"If a doll or other object had some emotional attachment to a deceased person, I cannot see why it is not possible for a human spirit to attach itself to the object. A spirit or a demon can possess an object including a doll. If the doll was used for some kind of rite, or ritual that was for occult purposes or Satanic purposes, the object could become possessed."

Sometimes events that take place in the presence of a doll (or other item for that matter), can create a certain air about it that is unsettling. Take the case of the doll that bore witness to acts of cannibalism.

In 1846, a young girl named Patty Reed was carted off by her family as part of a pioneer group heading west. The group would later become famous, or rather, infamous, as "The Donner Party."

During the difficult journey west, eight-year-old Patty was told to get rid of all her toys and unnecessary items. The heavy load needed to be lightened, and despite the difficulty of such a task for a young child, she complied. Mostly. Patty managed to keep her beloved doll, hidden beneath her voluminous dress. The doll was small, at only four inches, so although Patty herself was small, she was able to keep her special toy well hidden.

What unfolded for the pioneers was a horrifying struggle for survival. Trapped and snowbound with little hope, the settlers had to spend months stuck in the high Sierras with no provisions. The desperate travelers started eating anything they could in order to hold on to life. Leather items, old bones, and eventually…the bodies of those who died.

Depending on one's viewpoint, the story of the Donner party is a macabre tale of horror, or a noteworthy struggle to live. Whatever the case, Patty Reed and her family miraculously survived and made it to California. She lived a comfortable life in San Jose and her doll stayed with her.

Today, the antique doll that witnessed the struggles of the Donner Party is on display, tucked safely in a glass case at Sutter's Fort State Historical Park Museum in Sacramento, California.

While there are no current accounts of paranormal activity around the doll, many people who visit the museum and see the item find it extremely creepy. As one woman who viewed the doll stated:

"I haven't heard anything about it being haunted, but God, you'd think if any doll was haunted that one would be! I mean, that creepy little thing watched people eating people, there's got to be something imbedded in it."

John Zaffis, the "Haunted Collector," says many people unconsciously pick dolls that have attachments or contain strong spirit energy. Zaffis, along with co-writer Rosemary Ellen Guiley, discuss dolls briefly in their book, "Haunted by the Things You Love." Regarding people who buy haunted dolls unintentionally:

"…some were collectors, and their emotional high at adding a "find" to their collection probably canceled out any warnings from their intuition. With others, it was often a moth to flame story. Some people were unconsciously drawn to the paranormal. If there was a haunted object available, they managed to find it, usually without realizing it. Their problems then ranged from mild hauntings to life-threatening possessions and take-overs."

Zaffis has gathered haunted objects for years. Some from cases he's called to work on, other times, the items are sent to him anonymously. Often, people come to realize an object is cursed, haunted or possessed and just want rid of it as quickly as possible. John's vast museum contains countless objects, and as stated previously, more dolls than anything else. Like others who deal with haunted items, Zaffis reminds people:

"The fact that objects can house spirits or energy may seem fantastic, but it's ancient knowledge. Our early ancestors, who cultivated relationships with the spirit world, figured out that just about any object can be turned into a bridge to otherworldly realms.

Any object has the potential to acquire spirits and forms of energy, however—no rituals required. Daily use and emotional attachments, such as having a fondness for a particular favorite object, can imbue an item with sufficient energy to produce types of haunting phenomena later on."

John's statement "no rituals required" may seem to negate the argument that magical imbuing of a dolls must be intentional, but there are many ways a doll, or other object can become alive, and dolls specifically fit the bill for numerous types of energies and attachments.

In "The Collector's History of Dolls," Constance Eileen King recounts the odd tale of a middle-class couple and their strange relationship with a Victorian doll:

"The doll has its own chair, table, and crockery, and is changed into a night-dress at night. It has a wardrobe of lovely period dresses for day wear and a trunk to keep them in. Though admitting to being slightly afraid of the doll, which they have called Unity, they have created a daily ritual connected with looking after the effigy child, and they are deeply concerned if they break the ritual by coming home late from a dinner party."

In the lives of some, a doll can exert a powerful, almost primitive force that may be difficult to reckon with. At the least, the family in this account felt their doll was alive, or possessed of consciousness, and as a result, they poured constant mental and emotional energy into it. King's book was written in the 1980's and the account collected sometime prior to that. It would be interesting to know where this doll is now and if it's surrounded by reports of paranormal activity.

Sometimes, the intent to treat the figure as a living being is a conscious one from the start. King relates another account, passed on to her by a dealer who ran a shop specializing in dolls and accessories. According to the account:

"...one customer visited her shop each week and began by buying Victorian baby gowns and christening robes. Another week she bought an Edwardian dolls' pram, and on another occasion a cradle. The dealer had failed to connect the purchases, thinking the woman to be a toy collector, until one day, very cheerfully, the customer arrived and stated that today she would buy the life-sized baby doll!"

On other occasions, there are cases that imply other, outside forces are at work in the supernatural behavior of dolls. Take the case of the Bowman family.

In 2008, the Bowman's bought a special gift for their two-year-old son James. The "Elmo Knows Your Name Doll" is a toy of the popular, furry red figure from Sesame Street. The doll is programmed to recite its owner's name, along with various other personalized phrases. Not only did the talking Elmo know James's name, but it somehow developed a darker vocabulary. Much to the distress of the Bowman's, their son's new toy started repeating threats. Elmo would gleefully cry out "Kill James!"

Oddly, the toy only started using such phrases after fresh batteries had been put in it. No one in the family was responsible for the terrible phrases, and James's mother became understandably distraught. She hid the toy away out of her son's sight and contacted the manufacturer. Fisher-Price, the company who produced the toy could offer little explanation but did offer a voucher, so the item could be replaced.

Weird mechanical glitch, disturbing prank, or was a negative force at work? Too often, we just aren't able to answer such questions, but there are many traumatized adults and children who have unsettling memories connected to dolls. Anne McLaughlin is a good example.

Anne grew up with a display cabinet filled with dolls, including a set of wooden nesting dolls and a dancer doll. But one particular figure always stood out:

"One of the dolls in the cabinet was absolutely terrifying. Very tall, thin doll and her face was not a doll face. It was a grown woman, so she didn't have big eyes, she didn't have a smile. She had tiny little eyes. She always looked like she stepped out of one of those New Orleans ghost stories."

McLaughlin explains that the doll was also a music box and sat on a stand. When wound, the doll would spin slowly as the music played. The girl always found the doll bothersome and she was frightened of it. Despite the fear, she decided to take the doll out one night. An attempt, perhaps, to prove to herself that the doll wasn't really scary. She wound the doll, put it on her bedside table and walked away. Just as she did, there was a crash:

"And right when I turned around, she had just walked to the side of the

31

bedside table, and fallen to the floor with a big crash."

McLaughlin was so disturbed she quickly left the room.

"I went and slept with my parents."

The next morning, the girl went back to her room. She was done with the doll. She mustered her courage and put it back away in the cabinet.

"I was really sure to put her in the cabinet facing away from me...so that she couldn't watch me."

It seems it's the nature of children to have dolls. As Victor Hugo wrote:

"In the same way as birds make a nest of anything, children make a doll of no matter what."

Likewise, it seems by nature, strange energies will often find their way to dolls. Whether they are objects that are loved and cared for, or whether they are objects used as focal points of nasty, vindictive energy, dolls will forever be easy vessels for energies that for now are beyond our complete understanding.

Voodoo Dolls

The doll is made of cloth, usually black in color. There's a painted-on face and on top of the head, some hair, sometimes fashioned from yarn or string, sometimes human. A scrap of clothing is attached to the doll, something obviously cut from another garment. The doll is riddled with pins, fiercely driven into the head, heart and intimate regions.

This is the classic Voodoo doll.

Voodoo dolls are a vast topic in and of themselves. They are easily the most well-known magical dolls in the world. They also have one of the most confusing origin stories. While many people are still under the impression that Voodoo dolls are of strictly African genesis, they are actually a new world creation. Part of their origin in fact, lies in European tradition where "poppets" were used in sympathetic magic to inflict harm on targets. Settlers traveling from various points in Europe carried these ritual concepts with them to the United States during the colonial period and beyond.

During the period of the slave trade, a melting pot of cultures was created. Slaves taken from West Africa were thrown together with people from other parts of Africa and the Caribbean. In places like New Orleans, various folk and magical traditions blended together and began to evolve. The idea of European poppets, the concept of African fetishes and magical practices from Haiti somehow morphed into what is commonly recognized as the modern Voodoo doll.

There's no doubt the use of dolls for magic took hold with slaves in the deep south. The Africans among them recognized the idea of an image as a magical focus from their use of "bocio" in their native land. Bocio are effigies designed to be mediators to the spirit world. Bocio could be used to contact ancestors and deities to obtain protection, healing and other assistance. In this case, the doll, or bocio itself, was not the source of power, rather it was simply a vessel through which communication with other powers could occur. Considering their level of suffering, it wasn't much of a leap for slaves to transition to the use of dolls to curse their enemies.

Antique dolls from the 18th and 19th centuries have been found on several plantations in Louisiana. They bear some resemblance to traditional African bocio, but they are bound with twine or sometimes catgut, and stuck through with pins or small fish bones.

By the 1930's and 40's, movie makers jumped in and started using Voodoo dolls as a fearful image and plot device in films about Haitian Vodoo, further cementing the connection between the ritual dolls and island magical traditions.

Widespread interest in the occult in the 1960's and 70's saw a rise in Botánicas, shops catering to those practicing Afro-Caribbean traditions. By this time, Voodoo dolls had become a staple item. An article from the Monday, September 15, 1969 edition of the *New York Times* gives some insight into the common availability of "black rag dolls" for magical use:

"Where Religion and Superstition Mix in the City."

"The blending of Christianity and superstition has produced a flourishing business for 'botánicas'—stores that at one time sold only herbs but that today do a thriving business in amulets, statuary, perfumes and candles.

Handmade poppet. Photo courtesy of Gerald Vance

They cater to Puerto Rican, West Indian, Cuban, Dominican and other believers in 'espiritismo,' or spiritism, which holds that spirits summoned from another world have a direct effect—for good or evil.

Its roots are deep in the religions and beliefs of the African slaves who were brought to the New World, as well as in the practices of the Indians and Spanish and French colonists in the Caribbean.

Practitioners of spiritism say there is great similarity between their beliefs and those of the traditional religions. They point to angels, devils, saints and holy spirits as manifestations of the spirit world…

"Our beliefs are not different, said Carmelo Ramos, who operates a botánica…We are just traveling different roads to reach the same goal."

While Mr. Ramos prefers to cater to persons who are seeking the help of 'good' spirits, he does not turn away those who seek to cast spells or to delve into 'black magic.' For them he has vials of 'bats' blood,' 'snake oil,' 'graveyard dust,' as well as the bones of various animals and candles in a variety of shapes.

Mr. Ramos also has black rag dolls (at $5 and $6), which are often sold along with a gold-plated sewing needle. The needles are stuck into the dolls to cause pain and discomfort to enemies."

"Voodoo dolls" are now known around the world and are firmly attached to Voodoo and Haitian and African traditions.

In her book, "Voodoo Dolls in Magick and Ritual," Denise Alvarado states:

"…the foremost reigning icon of African-derived religions in the minds of the Western world is the Voodoo doll. Standing at the crossroads as a psychic link between the world of Spirit and the world of the mundane, Voodoo dolls provide a frightening glimpse into the world of the supernatural."

Alvarado continues:

"Very few things have the potential to create as much fear, panic, and paranoia as the discovery of a Voodoo doll lying on the front steps of home sweet home."

Today, in New Orleans, Voodoo dolls are sold in shops all over the city. They are popular novelties, a souvenir of old traditions from a city that lives and breathes magic and Voodoo.

Most of the dolls now found for sale are mass produced in places like Taiwan, a knockoff curio that comes complete with a package of pins and basic instructions. An appealing treasure perhaps, for those who want to cast some misery on one they feel wronged them.

The dolls are big sellers, a unique treasure from the land of Voodoo. In reality, most of the dolls sold end up as kitschy shelf displays, or pitched aside in a dresser drawer, a forgotten knickknack.

A few practitioners do still make Voodoo dolls by hand. Special, almost artistic items, such dolls can be found mostly in shops specializing in Voodoo and African arts. One local notes:

"Oh, there's still a market for the handmade dolls that look human-like. People come in on a regular basis and get them made to order, certain hair colors and so forth. And we frequently get questions about exactly how to use the dolls, especially when it comes to romance. People use them to get revenge on rejected lovers, and they use them to try to attract or control people they desire."

As always, in New Orleans there's magic above and below the surface, and the spirit of Voodoo, in all its forms, is alive and well.

Dolls & the World of Magic, Possessions & Hauntings

The Strange Art of Ventriloquism

Ventriloquism, also known as ventriloquy, is an <u>act of stagecraft</u> in which a person (the ventriloquist) changes his or her voice and "throws" it, so it sounds as if it is coming from another location, usually a doll or "dummy."

The now classic figures used by ventriloquists are technically known as "ventriloquial figures," and more commonly called "dummies." The figures range in size from twelve inches tall to human-sized, with the average falling between thirty-four and forty-two inches.

The art has a long, strange, and sometimes dark history. The term ventriloquism itself comes from the Latin root words venter (belly), and loqui (speak); in other words, "to speak from the belly, or stomach."

Originally, ventriloquism was connected to various religious practices. The Greeks called the art "<u>gastromancy</u>" and believed the voices produced by the stomach were actually spirits of the dead who had taken up residence in the stomach of the ventriloquist. They believed those with the ability were in contact with the spirit world, and, as a result, could speak to the dead and foretell the future.

The Pythia, high priestess at the temple of Apollo in Delphi, was one of the earliest recorded prophets to use the technique of gastromancy. The priestess acted as a conduit for the famous Delphic Oracle and doled out prophecies to heads of state, military leaders, and the elite in the ancient world.

Curiously, the Greeks considered Delphi itself to be the "navel of the world," making it somewhat fitting that "belly speakers" would be seated at the mystical location. The Oracle at Delphi was consulted about countless important decisions throughout the ancient classical world, and the information received carried a lot of weight.

An early "gastromancer," or prophet, at Athens named Eurykles was so popular and successful that gastromancers came to be referred to as "Euryklides" in his honor.

Other parts of the world also developed ventriloquism for ritual and religious purposes. Historically, adepts have been found in India, Africa, and various parts of Europe. The Maori, Inuit and Zulu people all have records of the art's use.

The art of ventriloquism has also long been associated with necromancers, those whose practice involves working with the dead.

By the middle ages, thoughts on ventriloquism were very different. The art was considered a manifestation of black magic and associated with witchcraft and Satanic rituals. Those who practiced ventriloquism during this period ran the risk of being burned at the stake, or hung.

Eventually, ventriloquism began to shift away from the strictly spiritual and religious use and towards entertainment. In the eighteenth century, the art was on display at traveling fairs and in market towns. The earliest known example of this dates back to 1753 in England where Sir John Parnell was depicted in an engraving performing the art and "speaking" via his hand. By 1757, a small doll was incorporated into a ventriloquism performance by the Austrian Baron de Mengen.

Ventriloquist performances were a well-established form of entertainment in England by the 18th century. Englishman Joseph Askins advertised his "curious" dialogue between himself and "Little Tommy," his invisible familiar.

It was an Irishman, one James Burne, who began to actively incorporate a doll in his performances on a regular basis. Records state that Burne "...carries in his pocket, an ill-shaped doll, with a broad face, which he exhibits...as giving utterance to his own childish jargon."

Englishman George Sutton incorporated a puppet into his act in the 1830s, but the man regarded as the true pioneer of modern ventriloquism is Fred Russell. In 1886, Russell took on an engagement at the Palace Theatre in London. His act was based on a "cheeky-boy dummy" name "Coster Joe." Russell would hold the dummy in his lap and engage in a dialogue with it. His act was highly influential and generations of performers that followed in his footsteps continued the

39

tradition of holding their dummies and having amusing conversations with them.

The British Heritage Society installed a plaque at one of Russell's former residences, noting his significance to the art. The plaque reads: "Fred Russell the father of ventriloquism lived here."

By the 19th century, the art had fully shed its mystical trappings and moved firmly into the world of performance art and entertainment.

For a time, the art of ventriloquism as entertainment thrived. It was well suited to stage and live performances. The art even thrived in the early days of television with notables like Edgar Bergen and Señor Wences. It waned however as taste in entertainment changed. Perhaps the modern world and its extravagant digital and audible effects made the art less impressive and magical, though some recent performers such as Jeff Dunham have become notably successful.

Trevor Cox, a professor at the University of Salford, teaches acoustic and audio engineering. In a 2013 article, he wrote about the ability of Ventriloquists to "trick" the human brain. According to his paper:

"This illusion happens because there is an area of the brain that processes both sound and vision, allowing what you see to influence where sounds appear to be coming from."

Scientists have studied the responses to ventriloquism to learn more about the brain's activity and the responses of the five senses. According to Jennifer Groh, a neurobiologist at Duke University in Durham, North Carolina:

"The prevailing wisdom among brain scientists has been that each of the five senses—sight, hearing, smell, touch and taste—is governed by its own corresponding region of the brain. Now, we are beginning to appreciate that it's not that simple."

Ventriloquist dummies have been popular figures in literature and entertainment. "The Horrible Dummy" by Gerald Kersh and "The Glass Eye" by John Keir Cross are two notable examples of stories involving dummies. Movies and television shows that have played on the fear of ventriloquist dolls include The Twilight Zone, Goosebumps, Dead of Night and Magic.

The art's long history aside, there's another aspect to address. The creepiness of ventriloquist dummies. Some people consider

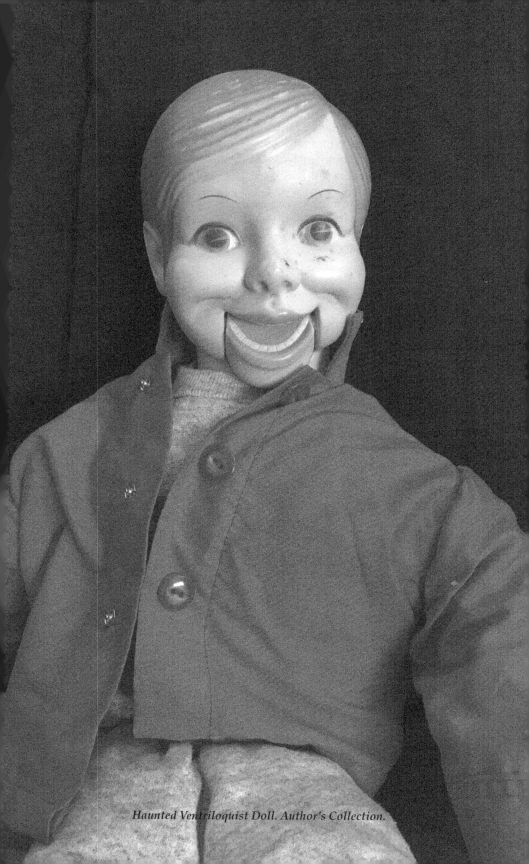

Haunted Ventriloquist Doll. Author's Collection.

them to be the most unsettling types of dolls with their moving eyes and ever-present smiles. The fear of ventriloquist dolls falls under the umbrella term, automatonophobia, loosely defined as a fear of wax figures, humanoid robots, audio animatronics, or other figures designed to represent humans.

Ventriloquist dummies can be even more disturbing since they "speak," again, perhaps, representing something just a little too human that evokes the feeling of creepiness.

The Strange Art of Ventriloquism

The Haunted Doll Trade

*"NASTY PERVERSE POSSESSED DOLL! * EXPERIENCED, ADULT COLLECTORS ONLY!!!*"*

So declared a listing posted on eBay in the summer of 2013. The haunted doll up for auction was one of a number listed for sale on the popular auction site. As the listing continued, more notes of caution, and details were given on the doll's background and history. As the listing describes:

*"***WARNING EXTREMELY NEGATIVE DOLL POSSESSED BY SEXUALLY SADISTIC DEMON****

This doll is certainly not for the beginner or casual collector. Experienced, adult collectors only please.

She is one of a group of dolls I got from an estate sale of a woman who worked in the children's ward at Pennhurst Asylum, in Pennsylvania. The woman's name was Iva, she worked at Pennhurst for 3 years, clear up until its doors were permanently closed in 1987. She left a journal depicting many of the horrors these kids suffered on a daily basis.

When the hospital was closed, many employees took property with them. Iva chose to take several of the tattered dolls that were used to placate the poor kids. For some years, Iva kept the dolls in a box in her attic. After her dream house was built, she decided to put the dolls on display. This turned out to be a huge mistake."

It would be curious to know if the buyer of the doll ever followed up on the details offered by the seller. Pennhurst is a notorious haunted location, and there are likely records of former employees accessible. Such information would add much to the accounting of any activity attributed to the doll. The seller had several dolls up for auction, but was adamant about the intensity of this particular listing:

"This is definitely the worst doll of the bunch. She is a very actively haunted doll, possessed by what I believe to be a male demon. The doll's eyes follow you no matter where you are. She will switch position to continue watching you whenever you are in the room. She moves from where she is left, often ending up wherever you are.

At night, you will hear her running around the house, getting into things. She is sexually abusive to the other dolls I have. Very sexually sadistic nature, and unfortunately, not only to the dolls...I am willing to give full disclosure of the sexual nature to the winner of this doll. Please think it over fully before bidding, be sure you can handle whatever may happen, as I will not take her back! Be at least 18 years of age, and experienced in dealing with these kinds of possessions."

By the time the auction ended, eleven bids had been placed and the "nasty, perverse, possessed doll," sold for a final price of US $1,526.00.

With shades of the murderous Chucky in their minds, most people would steer well clear of a listing for an evil, haunted doll, even if the high price were not an issue. But the listing example above is not a solitary one. Exploring eBay, you'll find a wandering maze of endless items up for auction. From the mundane such as books, DVDs and clothing, to the unusual and obscure. Among the oddities and antiques, there's a bustling trade in haunted items, and the most popular items in this category are dolls.

Dolls that are purportedly haunted can go for anywhere from twenty dollars, to amounts in the thousands, depending on the market at the time, and the providence and back story of the item.

The popularity of haunted objects has seen a dramatic rise over the past ten to fifteen years, and the turning point can be traced back to the sale of the haunted "Dybbuk Box" sold on eBay in 2004. The box, actually a wine cabinet, was purportedly used to imprison a negative spirit. It was bought and sold several times via online auctions. It was eventually the center point of the 2012 horror movie, "The Possession" directed by Sam Raimi.

Perusing sales listings for haunted dolls, most of the current crop list details stating that the dolls frequently move on their own, emit sounds ranging from voices, to crying or screams, to weird laughter, and demonstrate other, various lifelike qualities.

Frequently, the listings contain statements relating to evidence

45

gathered while investigating the item. EVPs (electronic voice phenomena), and high readings on EMF meters seem to be the most cited.

In a report for National Public Radio, Jak Hutchcraft talked about the haunted doll trade, noting how surprising it was to see haunted dolls go for such high prices on auction sites like eBay and Etsy. Hutchcraft stumbled into the world of the haunted doll trade one night while exploring the "Everything Else" section of eBay:

"There was an advert for something which was a sadistic, perverted, haunted doll. It was this little, menacing-looking sort of troll."

Hutchcraft watched as bids on the item climbed, going quickly beyond a thousand dollars. He was both puzzled and intrigued, wondering why people would pay such high amounts for reportedly haunted objects, so he did some digging:

"Some people want to connect solely with the spirit. Some people buy them just for the doll because they're doll collectors and the spirited aspect of it is just a secondary thing. I thought it was baffling, really, because I can look past the ghost as long as it's a cute doll."

Of course, the average person is curious and wonders what would cause people to purchase haunted dolls.

UK based paranormal investigator Jayne Harris says there's an appeal of companionship for some new owners, and many simply want a vessel so they can connect with a spirit, any spirit. Other buyers have motivations that are more personal. As Harris states:

"There are some people who are interested because they don't have children of their own. They ask if I've come across any spirited children that are in limbo. Adopting a haunted doll isn't always the right course of action for someone in that position. There's a lot of pressure on me to get it right. I don't give them out to just anybody."

Hutchcraft's research took him into the world of a strange subculture, filled with those interested in the paranormal, and actively collecting reportedly haunted objects. While he was initially a skeptic on such matters, delving into the subject matter as intensely as he did, changed his opinion. His thoughts on owning a haunted doll reveal his thinking on the topic:

"I thought about it. But the thing is, the more it went on, the more it took over my life for about a year, really…and then I started to think, 'Will

my brain trick me into thinking it is haunted? Or something will happen when I get it.' And, to be honest, I didn't have the money to fork out—and I was a little bit scared!"

Nancy Oyola, an online doll seller from New Jersey, told an interviewer she got her start in the trade of haunted dolls when she inherited more than three hundred of them from her late grandmother's estate. She swears she's had paranormal experiences with nearly all the dolls. She chose to sell them because, as she states:

"People are fascinated by them. Many people who work with black or white magic are in need of a particular spirit to help them with their spells and rituals, so I can help."

Oyola sells primarily on auction site Etsy and maintains high ratings from satisfied customers who confirm the ghostly attachments on the items they purchase from her.

Collectors and buyers from all over the world actively trade in haunted dolls, and some amass huge collections over time buying dozens and dozens of dolls.

One eBay buyer, stated that over time, and countless dolls, she had encountered few that were active once she received them. Eventually however, she stumbled across one that did prove very active:

"...well, since she arrived yesterday, I have been sick to my stomach and very dizzy, unable to sleep and very shaky...I guess in all this time I have found a truly haunted active doll...The others as I said have had moderate activity with the exception of a few they were just pretty dolls, but this one is throwing me for a loop."

Ultimately, Hutchcraft came away from his research with a different viewpoint regarding the world of haunted dolls, more intrigued by the people than the objects themselves:

"I think what fascinates me most about the community is the people, not their dolls. Everyone I spoke to was sincere and—perhaps a little anticlimactically—pretty much completely normal. They just so happen to believe that the figures they have sitting in their homes are inhabited by the spirits of dead children,

At the heart of it, it's the believers breathing life into this international subculture. Ghosts might not exist if the right people weren't there to see them, and those in the doll-collecting community don't seem to mind that the lines between fact and fiction are sometimes blurred. And in fairness, why should they? Followers of religion all around the world put their faith in the make-believe, and that's widely accepted as a logical, sane thing to do. How is this any different?"

Some collectors of haunted dolls call their figures "spirit children." They claim the dolls are not malicious, but merely misunderstood. They believe the spirits inhabiting the dolls are simply wandering souls looking for a place to be at peace and feel protected.

Others simply start collecting for reasons beyond their conscious understanding.

In the summer of 2017, UK news sources circulated a story about a Devon resident named Barry Collingswood. The 63-year-old man received media attention because of his hobby—collecting dolls, many of which, he claimed, are haunted.

Collingswood found his first doll in a secondhand shop. Even he isn't sure why he started gathering the dolls:

"I wasn't the sort of person to buy dolls and I never had done before, but I went into an old shop and thought: Oh, that's a very nice old doll' only to be offered two more for free."

Barry's wife, Sarah, wasn't happy about the man's new-found hobby. When he showed up with the first doll, she didn't want it in the house. Sarah, who suffers from Multiple Sclerosis, told her husband she didn't even want to look at the item and that he should get rid of it immediately. When the man went to comply with her wishes, things took a strange turn:

"I know it sounds crazy, but I got up on the wall outside about to put the doll which was still wrapped in polythene in a bin, when a gust of wind unwrapped it and all of a sudden I was on the floor. There was a pane of glass which I almost put my wrist through. She must have sensed what I was doing and tried to kill me."

Collingswood kept the doll and in a brief time he amassed a collection of over thirty others. He believes at least ten of them are haunted. In time, his wife adapted to the odd collection and the dolls are housed in the couple's bedroom. While his wife adjusted, his son however, has not.

Eighteen-year-old Josh likens the collection to creepy toys from horror movies like Annabelle. The young man told reporters:

Haunted Dolls at Spooked in Seattle. Photo by author.

"During the daytime the dolls aren't so bad, but at night the mood in the house turns completely. I don't think all of them are haunted, but I do get quite creepy feelings from them and I sometimes feel as though they're watching me when I'm home alone."

The couple's daughter, 21-year-old Natasha, doesn't care for her father's strange hobby either:

"Every time I go home there's a new addition. Mum will send him out to get milk and he will come back with a new doll. We often don't know where he gets them from. At the start, my mum would have to throw a blanket over them before she could go to sleep but now I think they've both adjusted to the odd collection. I try to avoid them totally when I visit home."

Creepy dolls fill many haunted locations. Photo by author.

When Barry posted photos of some of the dolls online, he started getting information about some of them from psychics. He was led to a ghost app that he installed on his phone to allow the dolls to "speak" to him. He now has daily, paranormal encounters with the dolls. One of the dolls, dubbed "Clara" has proven especially anxious to communicate.

"I was told Clara was 13 years old from Manchester and she passed many moons ago from high fever. She prefers men to women as her mother was not nice to her and she likes pets, car rides and would prefer to have a scenic view out of a window instead of being cooped up in a room."

Collingswood says Clara doesn't like his wife and during one conversation, he and his wife and son all witnessed the doll's eyes turn to ignore the woman.

The incident was more than enough for Josh, who now hopes to move out of the house soon.

"Clara creeps me out the most ever since I saw her eyes move. It will be nice to be in a house where there aren't haunted dolls watching me. I'm hopefully moving out this year to live with a friend."

How do you know if the doll you're buying is legitimately haunted? The short answer is, you don't. There are no definite answers in the paranormal, and certainly within the realm of haunted objects, there are endless questions to be answered.

Ultimately, when it comes to buying a haunted item, especially from an online auction site, the caveat is buyer beware. You may end up with an object that has zero activity, or you may end up with something that brings chaotic paranormal energy with it.

The continued fascination expressed by ghost hunters and collectors alike looks like it will fuel the market for haunted dolls for many years to come.

A World Full of Strange Dolls

Japanese Curse Dolls

"All you brats jump from here and die."

It was September 26, 2017, when a group of children on their way to school found this note. It was attached to a straw doll, hanging from the railing of a pedestrian land bridge. The implications were clear. Someone wanted the children to meet a terrible end.

The straw doll, known in Japan as a "wara ningyo," is similar to a voodoo doll. It's used as an effigy to place a curse of ill fortune or death on its target. Someone was trying to use the power of the doll to make the children leap to their deaths.

The incident occurred near the Edogawa Elementary School in Tokyo and alarmed school officials contacted police right away.

In short order, authorities traced down the source of doll and note. The guilty party turned out to be forty-one-year-old Takeshi Inaba, a man living near the school. When confronted, Inaba told police:

"Those kids running wild in the park are too noisy."

It's believed Inaba is also responsible for a series of thirty letters sent to parents and staff members of Edogawa school. The letters complained about the adult's inability to control the "noisy kids." Additionally, the man was linked to graffiti found in a local park sprayed on benches and a public toilet. Messages included statements such as "Kids are too noisy!"

Inaba is facing charges of criminal intimidation. There's some debate as to whether or not the supernatural threat of the doll is actually criminal… however, it is at the very least, creepy. While

Inaba may not face serious legal consequences, he will likely end up spending time with a mental health examiner.

The use of straw curse dolls goes far back in Japan's history. They were used both to make wishes, and to harm or kill a person.

The Nara National Research Institute for Cultural Properties has a relic from the 8th century recovered at an archeological dig—a doll made of bound wooden strips with an iron nail shoved through the chest.

Some accounts trace them back to Japan's Edo period (1603-1868) where it seems the tradition became more widespread. However, earlier evidence goes back to the Heian period (794-1185 CE) when sorcerers utilized dolls for curses. Iron was a rarity at that time, so wooden stakes were used to pierce the dolls.

The use of curse dolls is not something taken lightly by traditional Japanese. Using such magic involved more than just grabbing a doll and shoving nails in it. A precise ritual had to be followed for the magic to work correctly.

The ritual has to be carried out during the "ushi mitsu," the "old double-hour of the ox." This is the period from one AM to three AM. A time when the spirits of the dead, as well as the gods and evil entities are alive and roaming about. The gods worshipped by both Buddhist and Shinto adherents can be petitioned at this time.

The curse ritual itself is performed at a shrine. While the practice is not openly condoned, many shrines have a reputation for being famous "cursing shrines." Kifune Shrine and Kiyomizu Temple in Kyoto are both well known for their long use by those placing curses. Many trees at these shrines show extensive damage from countless nails driven into dolls over the years.

It's important the ritual be kept secret. Special ritual clothing must be worn for the process. A white robe, white obi (belt) and white paint on the face. Around the breast is placed a round mirror, and on the hip, a sword is worn for protection. Wooden clogs with only one support are worn and the person performing the ritual must bite down on a wooden comb as they are not allowed to speak during the process.

Special headgear is also required for the ritual. The headpiece, "gotoku," is essentially the bottom of a tripod similar to those used

Japanese Curse Ritual. Public Domain illustration, 1779.

in hibachis, upside down, with its feet point up. On each of the three spokes is a lit candle.

The dolls are made from straw, in the shape of a human with arms, legs, torso and head. The curse is most effective when something belonging to the victim is integrated into the creation of the doll. Hair, nail clippings or blood work best as they all create an energetic connection to the intended target.

The doll is taken to a sacred tree at the shrine where long metal nails—specifically five-inch nails and a wooden mallet— are used to pin the doll to the tree.

The nails are driven into various parts of the doll, usually to represent where harm should befall. For maximum effect, the ritual process can be repeated seven nights in a row, with the seventh night culminating in a nail through the doll's head—and the death of the victim.

Even the journey to the shrine must be carried out carefully. If the petitioner meets someone else during the expedition to the shrine, the other, innocent person, might "catch" the curse and die instead of the intended victim. There are other risks involved in the ritual, too. If someone sees the ritual being performed, there is a risk the curse can rebound back to the caster. Furthermore, carrying out such a powerful curse and death magic threatens the soul of the caster and may lead to them turning into an *oni* (demon).

These days the rituals are still carried out, but with a photograph of the victim's face placed on the head of the doll. Much of the traditional ceremony has been discarded for expedience, but those attempting the magic still sneak into shrines and nail their curses to sacred trees.

In modern Japan, the use of death magic is not considered acceptable. It does not, of course, mean such rituals are not carried out. Ritual kits to cast the curse can be purchased online, often found on Amazon Japan and other mainstream sites. People caught carrying out rituals using the *wara ningyo* are often prosecuted by authorities.

A recent case in Kyoto involved a man caught after nailing a straw doll to a sacred tree. He was caught on shrine grounds after hours, and the doll had a photograph of a woman's face attached, along with her name. Nails had been driven into the doll's body to pin it to the tree.

After his arrest, the man stated he was angry at the woman after she had rejected his attentions. He wanted, he said, to "get even with her." Legal arguments against the man's actions include the implication that his actions were a form of intimidation and should not be taken lightly.

The Faceless Dolls of the Amish

The Amish. A mention of the term usually conjures up images of horse drawn buggies and simple clothing. Many people mistakenly think the term Amish is an ethnic identification, but the it's actually used to describe a religious group. The Amish are a group of traditional Christian church fellowships with Swiss Anabaptist origins that date back to 1693. By the early 18th century, many Amish emigrated to Pennsylvania. From there, they spread out to other parts of the United States and Canada. There are now notable populations of Amish in Pennsylvania, Ohio and Indiana. There are currently over 300,000 Amish in North America.

The Amish are known for their simple living, plain dress and their refusal to utilize modern conveniences and technology. Amish society places heavy emphasis on church and family relationships. They value rural life, manual labor and humility, and following the word of God in accordance with the Bible.

When it comes to the Amish, few people outside their society understand their values and beliefs, but their handcrafted furnishings and old-fashioned food have become popular among tourists. Shops and restaurants have sprung up in "Amish country," and they cater to both locals and visitors.

Along with the furniture and simple, farm-raised foods, Amish art has become a popular form of American folk art, including Amish dolls. But there's an unusual and unique aspect found on traditional Amish dolls—they have no faces.

The modern Amish dolls are a type of rag doll usually lacking physical features of a face or hair. Since the materials traditionally used to make the dolls are remnants from clothing made for family members, the doll bodies are commonly made from white or cream fabric such as unbleached muslin. Fabrics are all solid colored, and the clothing is fashioned in the image of clothing worn by the Amish themselves. The stuffing was traditionally rags, but usage of cotton, or in modern days, polyester batting, is also common.

Some older Amish dolls have several layers of cloth on the head and/or body of the doll. When a doll became too dirty or worn, it was often re-covered with fresh cloth. The dolls may be hand sewn, or made by machine. Machine sewing in the Amish community is usually done with foot-operated treadle sewing machines.

Both girl and boy dolls are common; Amish children do not have a lot of toys, so both genders play with the dolls.

But why are the dolls faceless? There are conflicting accounts, but one involves a young Amish girl who was given a rag doll with a face for Christmas. The little girl's father became upset and cut the head off the doll, telling his daughter: "Only god can make people." The man replaced the doll's head with a stuffed stocking that had no face and the girl played with the doll for many years after the incident. Other stories claim Amish children have been known to wrap blankets around small logs and pretend they are dolls.

A sociological study from 2007 stated that Amish dolls are left faceless because the culture believes that "all are alike in the eyes of God." The study cited the lack of facial features agrees with the Biblical commandment against graven images.

There are of course some variations of tradition and belief among the Amish. For instance, some will use technology in limited amounts, or on certain occasions. Likewise, there are some Amish who allow their children to have dolls with faces.

Although sources differ on the exact origin of this tradition, most historians believe these dolls are not faceless for any one reason, but rather several issues, which primarily relate back to strict Amish religious tradition. Not every Amish doll is missing a face, but the traditional ones are the most well-known.

When it comes to traditional, practical reasons for making the strange dolls, there are a range of reasons listed that reportedly explain why the Amish figures have no faces, which include:

Biblical reasons—According to the biblical book of Deuteronomy, people are forbidden from creating idols and graven images. The Amish interpret this teaching to mean that nothing should be created as an accurate representation of the human form. This includes objects like dolls. By creating a doll that is faceless, children will not carry and play with a graven image bearing human likeness, thus, avoiding any sin.

Equality—One of the most important tenets of Amish religious tradition states that all people are the same in the eyes of God and should be treated as equals. If a doll has no face, it is free of identity and reinforces the concept of equality within the community, and, in a larger context, the world at large.

Vanity—Amish religious precepts teach that pride and vanity are terrible sins. The Amish believe any representations of a person's likeness are forbidden since they encourage vanity. This is one of the reasons the Amish have provisions against photographs. In a similar vein, creating a doll with a human image is a depiction of an ideal human form and may encourage children to model themselves after the false image. Faceless dolls, it is believed, are an affirmation of modesty among the Amish.

Collecting—While most reasons for the faceless dolls are religious or traditional in origin, there is also an indication that commercial interests have provided a more practical reason. In the early 20th Century, several individuals started selling faceless dolls to collectors outside of the Amish community.

Wide interest in collecting Amish crafts began in the 1930s. In 1939, Cornelius Weygandt, a professor at the University of Pennsylvania, described his collection of Amish and Mennonite dolls, praising the "painstaking fidelity" of their costumes.

Among the Amish, most dollmakers were anonymous. An exception was Lizzie Lapp (1860-1932) of Lancaster County, Pennsylvania, who sold the dolls she made under her own name.

National advertisements for Amish dolls appeared in House & Garden magazine in 1941. These dolls have frequently appeared in souvenir shops near Amish communities.

In 1955, John A. Hosteler, an expert on Amish society, described the marketing of dolls to tourists as an aspect of the commercialization of Amish culture.

Although some Amish children are permitted to have dolls with faces, interest from collectors encourages sellers to continue making them with the traditional method. As a result, many traditional Amish seamstresses and doll makers will only make dolls with no facial features whatsoever.

Amish dolls have become highly collectible and can sell for upwards of one thousand US dollars. Reproductions have been widely produced, depressing the market.

Demonic Forces—there's another notable belief associated with the reason that the community's children play with faceless dolls. Not only are graven images forbidden by the Bible, but creating or possessing them opens a person up to the possibility of exposure to demonic forces.

A doll with the features of a human being could be a vessel for evil, and could be utilized as a residence for a demonic or negative entity. If a demon possessed a doll, it would be able to watch the people around it with the doll's eyes and observe with its other senses. Hence, dolls made without human qualities offer protection since the dolls have:

No ears—so they can't hear what is said.

No mouth—so they can never speak or whisper evil ideas.

No hands—so they can never clutch anything.

What may seem, on the surface, to be a silly superstition or primitive belief, represents one of the ways Amish society seeks to protect its children from the forces of darkness.

So remember, if you have ever seen a traditional doll of the Old Order Amish, bear in mind its curious lack of facial features may be a shield against the intrusion of dark forces.

Guatemalan Worry Dolls

The indigenous people of the Highlands in Guatemala created a unique version of magical dolls. According to the Mayans, worrying keeps people awake at night. In order to solve the problem of being plagued with worries and losing sleep, "worry dolls" were created.

The dolls are small, usually between one and a half to two inches tall. They are clothed in traditional Mayan costumes. The dolls are constructed with wire and wood, twisted into a frame to create the torso, legs, arms and head. Cloth and yarn are wound around the frame to fill the doll out and to add feet, hands and hair.

Often, little woven baskets and other traditional accoutrements are added to the dolls. They are usually sold in a set of six to twelve dolls in cloth pouches or wooden boxes.

As a remedy, when an individual is plagued with worry, they tell their worry to the dolls, one worry for each doll. The worry dolls are then placed under the pillow at night, giving the individual a peaceful night's rest. The next morning, the person awakens to discover that the dolls have taken their concerns away. A variation states that after telling the dolls your worries, you place them in their pouch or wooden box. The results are the same with the little dolls taking troubles away.

According to folklore, the origins of worry dolls lie in older stories about a magical doll that would grant a wish to the bearer. One traditional story says a "mysterious stranger" wearing a large hat, gave the secret of the dolls to a young girl:

"Tell these dolls your secret wishes. Tell them your problems. Tell them your dreams. And when you awake, you may find the magic within you to make your dreams come true."

Indonesia's Psychic Doll

Nina Consuelo Epton (1913-2010), was a British radio producer, broadcaster, and writer active in the 1950s and 1960s. Born in Hampstead to a Scottish father and Spanish mother, educated in England and France, Epton travelled extensively. She spent time in Europe, North Africa and Indonesia.

She was known to engage deeply with locals on her trips, and made it a point to learn about local customs. Epton was especially interested in magical traditions and mysticism. On her journey to the tropical island of Java in Indonesia, she found herself very compelled by the magical arts being practiced by people living in the "modern republic" of Java.

In her 1957 book, "The Palace and the Jungle," Epton chronicled some of her experiences on Java delving into traditions and folklore, including an experience at a "Ni Tuwong séance."

Epton had become friends with a young Indonesian named Arafa who assisted her in her search for magic on the island. It was he who approached Epton with the offer to visit a special ceremony in a small village.

The Ni Tuwong was a "magic doll," that Epton thought was a thing of the past. She was quite happy to have the opportunity to observe the ritual. As she recounts:

"I never would have thought that this curious custom had survived the revolution and the wave of modernism that followed it. Many more similar surprises were in store for me."

It was a Thursday, or, "Friday eve" as it is called in the Javanese calendar, when Epton and the young man made their way out to the site, a *kampong* (small hamlet) at the edge of a country town around 14 miles west of the city of Djakarta.

The magic doll ceremony was to be conducted in a cemetery. Epton paints a picture to set the scene as she and her guide traveled through sunbaked streets to a place shaded by huge coconut palms. Beyond the crude verandas of houses on piles, and the forms of sleeping peasants in sarongs, they made their way to the back of the kampong and to the cemetery:

"The cemetery lay at the back of the kampong, nearly a mile from the town. It was set upon a mound like a prehistoric tumulus, in the middle of gleaming rice-fields. Coconut palms formed a dense canopy over this peaceful oasis and an outer rim of cambogia trees spread fragrant cream blossoms above the plain Muslim tombstones. These cambogia trees are always associated with cemeteries in the country; they have no leaves and the twisted branches are the most lifeless-looking objects in Java, where no tree ever sheds its foliage."

Epton and Arafa saw several women and girls making their way to the cemetery over the ridges that separated the surrounding rice fields. Removing her shoes, as was the custom, Epton took up a place in the procession heading to the graveyard. Her feet sank to her ankles in the soft mud of the path.

Once in the cemetery, she found a group of old women under the tallest, straightest palms in the cemetery. The women were gathered together, bent over a tombstone, and were speaking in low, gravelly tones. As they spoke, they worked at arranging an object at their feet, impatient and fussy the entire time.

Another group, this one comprised of younger women, were seated nearby on the ground. Clustered together and sitting cross-legged, they waited with obvious excitement for the elder group to complete their preparations. The scene itself was magical, a glimpse of a tradition from the past:

"Faint wisps of incense rose from little brass bowls placed round the tombstone, which had been filled with the rose petals and pandan leaves used for offerings to gods and to the spirits of ancestors."

The old women finished their work around the tombstone and gathered around the objects of their attention. Two of the women bowed their heads and began to chant a mournful incantation. The focus of their ceremonial words was now visible to all in attendance; a doll that was about to be animated by spirits called *Ni Tuwong*.

"The doll looked as grotesque as a Guy Fawkes effigy, with its coconut-shell head, upon which great white eyes had been outlined in chalk; bamboo brooms served for arms and the bamboo frame that passed for a body was wrapped in a sarong that had been specially "stolen" for the occasion. I do not know why this should be so, but Ni Tuwong must always wear a stolen garment."

Epton states that the ceremony is quite long and extensive. The group of elder women had been in the cemetery for a couple of hours before Epton herself arrived. In that time, they burned incense and recited incantations to prepare the doll and summon the spirits. It was the group of old women who determined when enough preparation had been done and the spirits were ready to enter the doll. The old women made a sign to Arafa to move forward, take the doll, and carry it down to the kampong.

He took the bundle in his arms and walked ahead of the group, a strange look in his eyes as if he was in a trance. One of the elderly women jumped up and joined the group "with the sprightliness of a tree squirrel" and fell in line behind Arafa. She held a mirror clutched closely to her breast.

The other elder women followed along behind her, continuing to chant the special incantations, and carrying bowls of incense with them. Epton was on edge as the procession continued;

"The atmosphere had become charged with electricity as before a violent thunderstorm. All the way from the cemetery to the edge of the kampong, where Arafa stopped and laid down the doll, I had the uncomfortable feeling

that there was an unseen presence among us."

Other people from the kampong came out of their homes and joined the ceremony now unfolding. People gathered around in anticipation as Arafa set the doll up against the trunk of a coconut palm. Bowls of incense were arranged around the base of the tree. Silence fell over the crowd:

"All chatting ceased as one of the old women held the mirror in front of the stolid coconut head which stared uncomprehendingly at its reflection. Set down in writing, cold, after the event, this scene may sound absurd, but it was not; it was uncanny.

Could the shadow of a passing butterfly have been responsible for the change of expression that came over the doll's coconut face? For there was no doubt it had altered. It was not a dead and inert object any longer. The lumpy, fibrous head began—almost imperceptibly at first—to loll first to one side, then to the other."

Epton watched as the old woman with the mirror began to speak to the doll in low tones. Affectionate and urging, attempting to get further response from the formerly inanimate object.

As the crowd watched, the doll's head turned away from the mirror to look at the crowd of girls gathered around it. But it wasn't merely a small movement of the head, the doll's broomstick arms also began to move, twitching convulsively. Satisfied, the old woman lowered the mirror and spoke quietly to the crowd of gathered girls. The girls began to whisper among themselves until one finally raised her voice and addressed a question directly to the doll.

The doll shook its head from side to side, answering the girl's question in the negative. The elder interpreted the response, the girl would not be married this year. Another girl spoke up, asking a question about her mother's health. Yes, the doll nodded, the woman would recover from her illness. Epton watched as the strange scene continued to unfold:

"The questions now came tumbling one after the other and the doll rolled its head and moved its arms quicker and quicker as if inspired.

Suddenly, Arafa bent over and put a question to it. 'Ni Tuwong,' he said—loudly enough for all to hear— 'Ni Tuwong, what new friend have we here today?' There was silence as the doll cocked its ludicrous head to one side. Then, to my horror and amazement, it bent forward and pointed one of its long, skinny broomstick arms straight at me!

Everybody turned to look. Mesmerized, I stared back at the blank coconut face 20 feet away from me and felt the blood being drained from my cheeks. Ni Tuwong had leant forward so abruptly that she toppled over. She remained quite still, face downwards, with arms outstretched. 'She has left us — it's all over,' sighed one of the girls."

The spirit having departed, the crowd began to disperse, returning to their homes with revelations fresh in their minds. Glasses of tea were passed around to those who remained at the cemetery. Everyone seemed to ignore the now lifeless doll that lay unmoving under the tree.

Epton's mind was still reeling from her unusual experience when her companion approached her:

"Arafa came over to sit beside me. He was laughing. 'Don't you think that final act was cute?' he said in his American English. I could not bring myself to laugh with him. In spite of the heat, I was shivering violently. 'We must be going — it's getting late,' I said. 'By the way,' cautioned Arafa, 'there's no need to tell anybody in Djakarta about Ni Tuwong. They don't believe in her, you know.'"

Epton's curious telling is one of the only modern accounts we have of the Ni Tuwong, Indonesia's magic doll. Are these ceremonies still being performed in quiet, rural areas of the country? Perhaps at this moment, somewhere in Java, an animated doll is predicting the future.

Beating the Dolls

There's a strange festival celebrated in Northern India in the state of Uttar Pradesh. It involves the worship of snakes—and the beating of dolls.

According to the Hindu calendar, Shravan Maas is the most auspicious month of the year. The month is calculated astrologically and falls between July and August. The festival falls on the fifth day of Shravan Maas.

During the day, elders worship the lord of serpents. Milk is offered to snakes, as well as coconut sweets. Any activities that may inadvertently harm serpents is avoided. Married women observe a fast to bring good fortune to their families. Unmarried women fast to attract a husband. Women also spend their time applying mehndi, singing traditional songs and creating and playing with dolls.

Boys and men indulge in various activities and offerings.

Traditionally, women create dolls for the festival using old clothing and rags. In the evening the women gather together, adorned in new clothing, bangles and mehndi on their hands and travel to a crossroads. Once there, the women throw the dolls down and wait for the arrival of the male group. Men between the ages of 18-25 arrive on the scene carrying colorful sticks and proceed to beat the dolls. The women stand and watch as the dolls are beaten to pieces.

There are numerous stories that claim to be the origin of the beating of the dolls. The oldest account tells the tale of a golden kingdom in India's past. The kingdom was so wealthy and peaceful that leaders in surrounding kingdoms became jealous. In spite, black magicians were sent to the golden kingdom to bring about its fall. Dark things began to take place in the once beautiful region. The king called for his own magicians and they discovered the ploy that was unfolding. The magicians devised a way to rid themselves of the black magic adepts. The king's chief magician had dolls made, one for each of the black magicians running loose in the golden kingdom. He ordered the dolls beaten, stating that once the dolls had been "beaten to death," the dark magicians would be defeated and flee. The process was successful, and the golden kingdom returned to its previous state of peace and glory.

According to this tradition, dolls are made and beaten each year in imitation of the golden kingdom's magical ritual. Modern believers use it as a way to drive off any evil powers lingering about that could affect their families.

This aspect of the festival is viewed poorly by modern activists who say the doll beating is symbolic of violence against women, a serious issue in modern India. These people want the celebration ended or transformed. Activist Rashmi Sinha has been working to change the doll portion of the festival from *"gudia peetna"* (beating the doll), to *"guida jhulana"* (swing the doll). The organization she works for has had some success in recent years and some regions now keep dolls on swings for the celebration. Instead of beating the dolls, boys now push the swings as a way to celebrate and honor females.

La Isla de las Muñecas

Two hours from Mexico City, buried deep in the canal system, there's a bizarre island. For many years, locals avoided it. They said it was haunted, perhaps cursed. It's known as "La Isla de las Muñecas," or, The Island of the Dolls.

The legend of the island lies in the mysterious death of a young girl who drowned in the canal, and the man who became obsessed with appeasing her restless spirit.

In the 1940's, Don Julian Santana was a married man with a small family, living quietly in the coastal region of Mexico. No one knows exactly why, but in 1950, Don Julian suddenly left his family and the world behind, and moved to a small island deep in the canals south of Mexico City. The island became Don Julian's home for the remaining fifty years of his life. Although he remained married, he rarely saw his wife and children and never brought them to the island. On the surface, he appeared to simply be a man seeking solitude.

Locals in the area respected his reclusive nature, but noticed odd behavior. Don Julian was often seen digging through trash heaps and garbage dumps when he visited nearby towns. He wasn't digging for food scraps, clothing, or other necessities though. Don Julian was looking for dolls. The man would scavenge any doll, or portion of a doll he could find. Furthermore, he made great effort to barter for dolls on each of his visits to the mainland. He would bring fresh fruits from his island, and other items he had acquired, and bargain for dolls, carting them off when he returned to his home.

Curiosity finally got the better of a mainland resident who asked the man why he was so focused on obtaining dolls. The answer was both surprising and unsettling.

Don Julian told the man his island was haunted by the ghost of a little girl and she was taunting him. He believed the only way he could appease her spirit was by bringing her dolls. The story spread like wildfire, and soon the legend of the island of the dolls began to spread.

Over time, the island became overrun with dolls and pieces of dolls. They hang from trees and dangle from the limbs, attached with twisted metal wire and threads. They sit in the gnarled crooks of trees, high in the air, and they are buried in the base of trunks. They cover the forest floor in some areas. Some have been there so long that vines and weeds have taken them over causing a weird marriage of roots, vines and plastic. Sometimes, there's only a piece of a doll visible, leading one to wonder if the complete thing is even there. Glass eyes can be seen peering out from plants, moss and dirt.

Natural decomposition has added its touch to the bizarre gallery of grimy toys. Many of the dolls are cracked and decayed. Some of the faces look agonized. Animals and insects have plucked at the false hair, often leaving only tufts sticking off to move in the wind. The sun has created blisters on plastic faces, and over time the rain has worn away outer colors, leaving some dolls with a skeletal-like appearance. Exotic spiders and other insects have made many of the dolls their homes, crawling in and out of plastic limbs and torsos. A dirt path cuts through the vegetation, leading to the run-down shack where Don Julian spent much of his time, a primitive shelter that's also covered inside and out by dolls.

The island's current caretaker, a member of Don Julian's family, states:

"There are many stories that tell why the dolls are here. Some of the people believed that Don Julian was mad, but I don't believe that. When he first came to the island, he started to believe that the spirit of a young girl was here. She had drowned in the canal nearby and just after that he found the first doll floating in the water. He fished it out and tied it to a tree near the water to make the dead girl happy. He felt it would protect him from any evil. Soon, he felt he had to add another doll, and another. It just never stopped."

The dolls are said to be haunted, possessed by a spirit, or spirits, unable to find peace. Locals believe the restless specters lure the unwary to their deaths.

Don Julian himself passed away in 2001. Even his death is a mystery. After he hadn't been seen in town for some time, locals gathered their courage and went to the island to check on him. They found his lifeless body lying in the water in the same spot where he claimed the little girl had drowned. Adding to the strange mystery of his passing, no cause of death has ever been listed. Some believe he died of a heart attack, while others feel more sinister, unearthly forces were at work.

Over the years, numerous film segments have brought further attention to the island and its strange tale. Anthony Bourdain's "No Reservations," Josh Gates' "Destination Truth," and popular paranormal show, "Ghost Adventures," have all journeyed to see the dolls, and in the case of the last two, to investigate potential paranormal activity. In the wake of the popularity, other ghost hunters and curiosity seekers have made their way to the island to see the curious site. For many years, locals were hesitant to go to the spot for fear of tempting fate and being affected by the ghosts that haunt the place.

One man stated:

"I won't go near the place after dark. In the night, you can hear whispered voices, sometimes singing. The dolls talk to each other. They are possessed by restless spirits. They try to lure you in the darkness, hoping that you will drown. If you get close enough and if there is moonlight, you will see the dolls moving and you will see their eyes open and close."

The guide's comments echo a common theme in stories about the island. People say the dolls move around at will, not bound by the wires and ropes that seemingly hold them in position. Walking around, there's always the sense that perhaps something just moved behind you, or in the corner of your eye. Is it the wind causing the effect, or something else?

The island is difficult to reach and can only be accessed by *"tranjineras,"* canoe-like vessels brightly painted in vibrant colors; red, yellow, green, and white. The boats are propelled with a pole, gondola style, by their pilots. Those who do journey to the island are encouraged by locals to carry a doll, some candy, and white candles as offerings to the restless souls that haunt the dolls.

The Animated Dolls of the Myrtles Plantation

One of the creepiest stories about a haunted doll I've personally collected came from the Myrtles Plantation in the quiet little town of St. Francisville, Louisiana.

The Myrtles is a classic, pre Civil War, Antebellum plantation. Built in 1796 by General David Bradford, a journey to the site is a step back in time. Towering trees and a winding drive lead back to the home. There's a brick courtyard and a cool veranda with oversized rocking chairs that call out to visitors to sit and relax for a spell.

But classic architecture and inviting spaces aside, there's another fascinating aspect to the Myrtles—it's considered one of the most haunted houses in the United States. The historic home has been featured on dozens of paranormal programs, and is a popular "bucket list" location for ghost hunters from around the world.

It's also a popular Bed & Breakfast for those with an interest in the paranormal, as well as those interested in historic sites of the deep south.

The doll story in question was related to me by a man working for the Myrtles in the early 2000s. The creepy tale involved one of the porcelain dolls that sits on a bedroom mantle in the main plantation house.

One morning, the man saw one of the Myrtle's female guest downstairs and stopped to speak with her for a moment. He had seen the woman around the B&B the day before, and he knew she had checked in accompanied only by her small child. He looked around, and seeing only the woman, asked where the child was. The woman calmly replied the child was fine, but was sleeping upstairs in the stroller.

The man got very excited and told the woman she couldn't leave her child upstairs unattended. He rushed up the steps to check on the child. Entering the room, he received quite a shock.

There was the little one, fast asleep in the stroller, but, standing next to the stroller, was a doll from the mantle. One of the doll's hands rested on the side of the stroller, as if holding it. The man snatched the child out and rushed downstairs to report the incident.

The guest decided it was best to check out of the Myrtles.

There are other dolls in the historic Plantation home that are often the center of paranormal activity too. An old ragdoll in the William Winters Room is reported to suddenly leap off the mantle and fly across the room. Sometimes it "jumps" upwards towards the room's chandelier.

The Fannie Williams Room is nicknamed "The Doll Room." As the nickname indicates, it has several dolls, many of which are purported to be haunted.

A doll in the Ruffin-Stirling Room, the home's former nursery, is purported to vanish and reappear on a regular basis. It's believed the spirits of little girls take the doll to play and later return it to its position on the mantle. One investigator who stayed in the room swore there was no doll on the mantle at night, but the next morning, a doll had appeared, its shiny eyes staring out coldly. No one else had entered the room.

The Myrtles offers both historical tours and "mystery" tours that recount some of the ghost stories associated with the home.

At times, it's hard to separate the site's rich history from the countless stories and folktales that have been added to its mythology over the years. Popular tourist information claims the home was the site of ten murders, that it was built on ancient Tunica Indian burial ground, and that at least a dozen ghosts haunt its grounds. The Myrtles is a place where history's lines become blurred with fanciful tales and the experiences of those who journey to the site in search of ghosts. Its dolls have become a vital part of the growing body of lore associated with the famous haunted house.

Eerie Companions | *David Weatherly*

Famous Haunted Dolls

Robert The Doll

He's the grandfather of haunted dolls. At well over a hundred years old, he's known far and wide as one of the most haunted objects in the world.

He's known as Robert The Doll.

Robert resides in a simple glass case at the Fort East Martello Museum in Key West, Florida. Robert is somewhat of a celebrity, and people come from far and wide to see him, take his picture, and, sometimes, to test the dark powers the doll is said to possess.

Robert, you see, has been blamed for a wide range of tragedies. Car accidents, job losses, health issues from minor concerns, to broken bones, and even severe illnesses. And there's more, Robert has caused relationship problems, heartbreaks, even divorces and a litany of other misfortunes.

But Robert doesn't just dole out ill fortune to everyone. The doll's curse is reserved for people who make fun of him, or those who take his picture without first asking permission.

Robert stands forty inches tall and is dressed in a sailor's uniform. He has small, shoe button eyes, and a rather spongy appearance. His worn face is only vaguely human, and he has what many describe as a smirk. He's covered with small nicks, the scars of age and time. He is stuffed with excelsior, or wood wool, made of slivers cut from logs.

Robert originally belonged to Robert Eugene Otto, an eccentric Key West artist who came from a wealthy and prominent family. Young Robert Otto received the doll as a gift for his fourth birthday. Upon receiving it, he promptly gave his own name to the doll and declared that from that time forward, the doll would be called Robert and that he would go by his middle name, Eugene, or Gene for short. From the moment he received the doll, Gene and Robert were inseparable. As Gene's constant companion, Robert even had his own chair at the dinner table and, each night, Robert slept beside Gene in his bed.

Key West, a place long known for its many eccentric characters, has long known the story of Robert and Eugene. As the legend grew over the years, locals recalled the unusual relationship the young man had with the doll.

As Fort East Martello Museum curator Cori Convertito notes:

"What people really remember is what they would probably term as an unhealthy relationship with the doll. He brought it everywhere, he talked about it in the first person as if he weren't a doll, he was Robert. As in he is a live entity."

By all accounts, once Robert was a part of the Otto household, things started to change. "Incidents" began to occur around the boy and his doll. Broken household goods, missing items, rooms in disarray…and in the aftermath of each incident, a resounding claim from the young Gene: *"Robert did it!"*

It seemed no matter what happened, it was always Robert who was up to mischief. On the surface, one would assume it was a simple matter of Gene making excuses for his own misdeeds. But in this case, the logical excuse didn't explain everything that was happening. Gene's parents said they could hear their child at night, having conversations with Robert. The odd thing was, they heard another voice answering. It was as if Robert the doll was talking back to the boy.

The Otto's tried to dismiss the strange things they were hearing. Perhaps, they thought, it was merely their son, using a different voice to pretend the doll was speaking back to him. As things in the home became even stranger, they began to second guess their assumption.

Other reports stated that whenever someone spoke badly about Gene in his presence, Robert's expression would change.

Through the years, as the boy grew, the doll was always close by. Then came the day Gene was old enough to go away to college. He left Key West, and Robert the doll remained behind at the family home. Gene attended fine arts schools in both Chicago and New York. He also traveled overseas to Europe and while spending time in Paris, he met a Boston native named Annette Parker. Parker was a renowned pianist and performed for elite audiences around the continent, including a command performance for the King of England.

Romance blossomed, and in 1930, Eugene Otto and Annette Parker were married. Eventually, the couple moved back to the United States, living for several years in New York.

Things changed when Gene's mother fell very ill. A worried Gene convinced his wife to leave New York and move to Key West so they could be close to his family. Annette wasn't happy about the change.

Once in Florida, the couple took up residence in a stately home known as "The Artist House." It was then Gene was reunited with Robert the doll. The older Gene picked up right where he'd left off— Robert was brought to live at the Artist's House and was given his own room upstairs in the home's turret. The room was even complete with furniture and toys built to match the size of the doll. As an article in Florida's *Sun Sentinel* described, Gene went out of his way to make Robert comfortable:

"He built a special attic room for Robert, complete with its own correctly proportioned furniture and toys. He would often go up to the attic to spend time with his doll, and it was about this time, in the 1940s, that stories about Robert began to leak out of the house."

A plumber doing work in the home heard giggling coming from behind him. When he turned around to find out who was there, he found only Robert the doll—who had moved from one side of the room to another. The plumber left the house never to return.

The legend of Robert began to grow. Kids walking by the home would often see the doll sitting by the window in a rocking chair. They also claimed Robert would appear and disappear, that he would move around to different windows and whenever they passed by, the doll was there, looking down on them. Many children started going out of their way in order to avoid walking by the house, thinking it better to stay away from the lingering gaze of the living doll.

While Gene was considered an eccentric—not very unusual in Key West—by some accounts he also became abusive in his later years. According to area resident Myrtle Reuter:

"A neighbor told me Anne told him that whenever Gene did anything

mean or hateful he always blamed it on the doll."

The doll, it seemed, still had as much influence on Gene in his later years as it did when he was growing up.

Gene's wife Annette was clear about her feelings, she couldn't stand Robert. She felt Gene payed more attention to the doll than he did to her. She continued to tolerate the situation however, and in 1974, Gene passed away. Annette packed Robert away in a trunk and tried her best to forget about him and the strange relationship her husband had with him. She moved to Boston leaving Key West and Robert the Doll far away.

Robert of course, didn't stay in the trunk. After Annette left the Keys, the legend of the doll continued to grow. People who visited the Artist House, or spent any time there, came away with strange stories about the doll. Accounts of the doll moving on its own. Voices, laughter, footsteps and other strange sounds and incidents all centered around Robert the doll.

Another story that ran in Florida's *Sun Sentinel* related an account from two men who rented the home in the mid 1970's. The men quickly learned the upstairs room was the domain of Robert and he was very active:

"There was constant noise coming from the room. Sometimes it was like little kids laughing and other times like someone rummaging around. When it first started happening we would go upstairs to check it out, but always found nothing. It was only after a half dozen times we realized the doll had moved. At first, we blamed each other and laughed it off as a practical joke. Sometimes the doll's head would be looking in a different direction, other times its arms were propped up around the chair, and once its legs were even crossed. It started happening with greater frequency and we realized this was no joke."

Myrtle Reuter ended up with the Artist House and by default became Robert's new caretaker. She watched over the doll for years, and in 1994 decided to donate Robert to the Fort East Martello museum in Key West.

When she donated Robert to the museum, Reuter confirmed there was paranormal activity around the doll. She recounted constant noises from the attic room, and how Robert moved around the house on his own. She also claimed that at one point, Robert locked her in a room. She'd had enough of the doll's antics and thought it best Robert

Robert the doll at his home in Key West. Photo courtesy of Chad Lewis.

be placed in the museum. At the least, the doll was an antique and connected to a famous Key West citizen.

One of the earliest legends of Robert's origin claimed the doll was given to Gene for his fourth birthday by the Otto family's Bahamian maid. According to the tale, the Otto's fired the maid, and in order to get revenge on the family, the woman cursed the doll using black magic. By this account, the doll was brought to life via the island Voodoo it was enchanted with.

The story was a popular part of the mythos of the doll for many years. Black magic was blamed for the strange life Robert had taken on. It would also explain the misfortunes that befell so many people who came in close contact with the doll.

While it's a compelling story, it hasn't held water. Once researchers started digging into the true origins of the unique doll, they proved the fanciful tale of a Voodoo curse was far from the source of Robert and his strange qualities.

Key West writer David Sloan, as well as researchers with the Fort East Martello museum, worked hard to uncover the true history of Robert, and it lead back to the Steiff Company. Steiff was the same toy maker that first manufactured a Teddy bear in honor of Theodore Roosevelt.

Findings indicate Robert was never intended to be sold as a toy, rather he was likely made as part of a set of window display items. Robert, they found, was probably made originally as a clown or jester, and used for a store window display in Europe.

Researchers also verified that Gene Otto's grandfather purchased the doll on one of his trips to Germany, a unique birthday present for his young grandson.

As for the sailor suit Robert the doll wears, the clothing was not supplied or manufactured by the Steiff company. It's likely the outfit originally belonged to Gene as a boy and proved to be just the right size for Robert.

Robert is quite at home at Fort Martello and since his arrival, visitors have flocked to the site to see the mischievous toy. The museum has also become a popular stop on local ghost tours. People flock from all over the world to see the famous doll. He's been featured on countless television shows, he's had his aura photographed and he's noted as the inspiration for a popular series of horror movies featuring a doll—Child's Play featuring Chucky. There was also a film that debuted in 2015 called "Robert the Doll," a direct attempt to capitalize on Robert's legend and the success of the Annabelle movies.

Somewhere along the way, it became known that Robert the doll had a sweet tooth and people started giving him candy. Sometimes it's even sent by mail. Museum staff recall a box containing eight bags of peppermints and a nice card sent to Robert. Other people leave gifts for the doll when they come to visit. Staff members frequently find sweets, money, and even occasionally—joints. Some visitors are apparently trying to help Robert relax. Museum director Convertito notes:

"It's completely inappropriate, we are still a museum."

Exercising caution, Convertitio says museum staff do not eat any of the treats sent to Robert.

At the museum, and online, fans of Robert can buy books, t-shirts with his image, coasters, even small replicas of the doll. He has his own entry on Wikipedia and even has social media accounts. People can—and do—write to Robert.

In fact, Robert receives a lot of mail. On average, about three letters every day. But most of them aren't fan letters, the bulk of them are letters of apology. You see, many visitors to the museum fail to show Robert proper respect. Some are even openly insulting to him, making fun of him or prodding him about his purported ability to curse people.

As a result, many of the letters that arrive beg for Robert's forgiveness and ask him to please lift whatever curse or negative energy he's placed on them. Convertitio says the museum probably has over a thousand letters, all of which are kept and cataloged in the institution's' files.

On occasion, Convertito answers the letters on Robert's behalf. She makes a point of answering any children that write to Robert, and she also responds to others that are especially poignant. She recalls one email from a girl who was being bullied at school.

"Gene always had that childlike temperament around him and we felt like Robert would want to be kind to children."

Sometimes people write and ask Robert for advice, and at times, they ask Robert to help them more directly with their problems by hexing people who are causing them trouble.

There's even a happy birthday letter to Robert from US President George W. Bush.

The museum always keeps a display of letters on the wall behind Robert's case so people can see examples of the mail Robert receives, it's part of the fascinating legend of the doll.

Convertito is Robert's official caretaker, and once a year a special checkup is done on the doll. Convertito and her team take Robert out of his display case and check every aspect of the doll for wear and aging. It's an important process since the doll's straw filled body and aged clothing and outer components may be susceptible to Florida's humid climate.

Of course, spending so much time in the museum, and around Robert, the big question Convertito frequently gets is whether or not she believes the doll is haunted. After all this time, she says she's still not sure:

"I don't know. I really don't. I've never had a bad experience with him. I've never felt uncomfortable. It's always been a very basic relationship and I have a job to do and I go and do it. And whether there's something to it or not, he just allows me to get on with my job."

But aside from the letters, there's plenty of other accounts that have come since Robert moved to the museum. For instance, there are frequent reports of electronic interference around the doll. Cameras, phones and other devices often freeze up or crash completely around Robert. People who dare take his picture without first asking permission usually suffer the worst effects, experiencing ill fortune and mishaps soon after the act.

Thomas Locklear, from Key West's "Ghost & Gravestones Frightseeing Tour," had his own incident with Robert. Locklear made the mistake of taking a photo of a new ghost tour guide next to Robert without first asking the doll's permission. He recounts:

"The phone I used got very hot and stopped working before I left East Martello. When I took it to Verizon the next day they said the entire inside of the phone burned up and they had never seen anything like it."

Locklear added:

"All of us who work with him (Robert) have, at the very least, seen his facial expression change. Most of us have seen him move."

Today, Robert sits on a doll-sized wooden chair in his own plexiglass case to protect him. The case however, hasn't stopped Robert from moving about. There are frequent reports from people who say they see the doll move, even though he is secured in his case. Reports also surface from people who see the doll's facial expression change.

There's yet another curious incident that has added to Robert's legend. Originally, he was alone in the display case, however, he now has a small, stuffed lion, nicknamed "Leo" sitting on his lap. The mystery lies in how exactly Leo came to be in Robert's display case.

According to a museum employee, the stuffed animal was once part of the Edna Wolkowsky dollhouse display housed in a separate case in the museum.

One day a volunteer was cleaning the display when she noticed a pronounced, empty space, between two of the stuffed animals in the cabinet. She checked the case and found it was still locked and showed no signs of having been tampered with. She made a note to inform the museum's curator about the oddity. As she continued with her cleaning, she made her way over to Robert's display area where she suddenly noticed the missing toy sitting on Robert's lap! The staff was puzzled by the incident. Some were even a little unnerved, but no human element could be found responsible for the teleporting toy. Museum staff left the stuffed lion alone and it has remained with Robert ever since.

It seems Robert didn't want to be in his case alone.

Annabelle The Haunted Raggedy Ann

"Warning, Positively Do Not Open"

So says the sign in front of an unassuming Raggedy Ann doll sitting in a specially made case in a museum in Connecticut.

Behind the glass is the doll Annabelle. She became internationally known after appearing in 2013's hit movie "The Conjuring" and has the headline in 2014's film "Annabelle." A sequel, "Annabelle:

Creation," was released in 2017.

Curiously, the doll in the movies is very different from the real Annabelle. Filmmakers apparently wanted a more disturbing doll than a simple Raggedy Ann, so they created a screen version made of porcelain with an unnerving, leering smile.

One of the things that has made the Annabelle films so popular is that they're based on an actual paranormal case, one originally investigated by well-known couple Ed and Lorraine Warren.

The Warrens rose to prominence after their involvement with the "Amityville Horror" case. A purportedly demonically haunted home on the south shore of New York's Long Island. The case was later made into a major motion picture, gaining it even more attention.

But the Warrens had been pursuing the paranormal for many years. In the 1940's, the couple began investigating homes reported to be haunted. In 1952, the Warrens founded NESPR, the New England Society for Psychic Research, a group established to investigate reports of paranormal activity and hauntings. The group is the oldest such organization in New England and utilizes a wide range of professionals, including law enforcement officers, medical professionals and more.

Well before their involvement with the Amityville case, the Warrens found themselves involved with the case of a haunted doll: Annabelle.

Annabelle's story begins in 1970 when a mother purchased an antique Raggedy Ann doll from a second-hand store. The doll was a birthday present for her daughter, Donna. At the time, Donna was a college student about to graduate with a degree in nursing. She lived in a small apartment with a roommate, another nurse named Angie.

Donna loved the doll and put it on her bed as a decorative item. Before long however, strange things began to happen. Donna and her roommate were convinced the doll was moving on its own. The movements were relatively unnoticeable at first, with only slight changes in the doll's position. But the more the women payed attention to the doll, the more noticeable Annabelle's movements became.

As the days passed, the movements became even more dramatic. Donna and Angie would come home and find the doll in a completely different room from the one in which they had left it. Sometimes, the doll would be found sitting on the couch with its legs crossed and its arms folded as if it was angry. Other times, the doll would be standing, leaning against a chair in the dining room. On several occasions, Donna placed the doll on the couch and when she returned, she would find the doll back in her bedroom with the door closed. Annabelle, it seemed, had a mind of her own.

Annabelle's movements weren't the only disturbing thing about the doll. About a month into the women's experiences with the doll, they began to find messages written in pencil on parchment paper. The hand writing looked like it belonged to a small child and the statements would say things like "Help Us." Even more disturbing was the fact that the girls didn't keep parchment paper in their apartment. Was Annabelle manifesting the notes out of thin air? No one knew where the paper with the strange messages came from.

One night Donna came home and again found the doll sitting on her bed. This time however, something was different. Inspecting the doll, Donna found what appeared to be drops of blood on the back of its hands and its chest. The women were scared and decided it was time to call in some experts. They needed to know exactly what they were dealing with, and if they were in trouble.

The girls contacted a medium, and a séance was held to find some answers. The psychic told Donna and Angie the doll was inhabited by the spirit of a dead girl named "Annabelle Higgins." The psychic said the Higgins girl had resided on the property before the apartments were built on the site. When the little girl was only seven years old, her lifeless body was found in the field where the building now stands. The little girl's spirit told the medium she was comfortable with the nurses and wanted to stay with them. In a sense, the women were somewhat relieved at the psychic's information. They felt sorry for the girl's spirit, so they gave her permission to remain with them and stay in the doll.

It was a big mistake.

The women may have believed they were dealing with the lonely spirit of a little girl, but whatever was inhabiting the Raggedy Ann, it was certainly not an innocent child.

In short order, things took an even darker turn. A friend of Donna's, a man named Lou, suffered a strange attack by the spirit in the doll and received a series of burning claw marks on his chest. The sudden physical attack helped Donna realize things were much

Zak Bagans & Annabelle. Photo courtesy of Zak Bagans.

more serious than she and Angie first thought. Reaching out for other opinions and help beyond the medium's input, she contacted a priest at the Episcopal church. After hearing the details of the case, the priest, in turn, contacted Ed and Lorraine Warren, known experts on occult and demonic matters.

The Warrens visited the home, interviewed the girls, and quickly determined demonic elements were at play. Ed believed a demon had taken up residence in the doll and everyone in the household was in serious danger.

Donna's home was cleansed and blessed, and the Warrens took Annabelle away. The drive back to their home was a perilous one for the Warrens. They later reported that at each curve, the car swerved and stalled, and the power steering and brakes kept failing. In the back seat sat Annabelle, the demon possessed doll.

Ed stopped the car and called on a higher power. He doused the doll with holy water and the car returned to its normal function. The Warrens then made it home safely.

Once they had the doll back at their home, the Warrens noticed it was still quite disturbed. The doll would levitate. At times, it would vanish from one spot, only to reappear elsewhere. The Warrens had a special case constructed for the doll and tucked it away in their museum of the occult, sealed with various spiritual protections.

Over the years, many people have had negative experiences connected to Annabelle, and the popularity of the recent films have made her one of the most well-known haunted dolls in the world.

Ed Warren passed away in 2006 at the age of 79. The Warren's son-in-law, Tony Spera, now handles the Warren's Occult Museum, which of course includes Annabelle. Spera says he learned directly from Ed over the years:

"...I listened to Ed tell the stories during his lectures, then we'd go on cases and he'd explain what was going on in the house. I was taught by the master of demonology...it was very, very frightening at the time, but very interesting too."

Spera occasionally hosts "An Evening with Annabelle" events that includes a dinner and a chance to meet the real-life haunted doll. Everyone is required to sign a waiver releasing the hosts from *"any liability or traumatic influence associated with viewing the items or being in the presence of Annabelle."*

The warnings don't deter anxious attendees, ready to see the famous doll and find out if they too have any unusual experiences from being in her presence.

In 2017, a rare investigation was conducted involving Annabelle. While Spera has long been reluctant to take the doll out of her case, or to allow it to be away from the safety of the museum for very long, he agreed to take Annabelle on a special journey for Halloween.

Spera and the doll flew to Las Vegas, Nevada to appear on the Ghost Adventures Halloween Special. The event took place at Zak Bagans' Haunted Museum. Annabelle was brought to the location in a special carrying case. Tony Spera removed her while wearing heavy gloves, one of his methods for protecting himself from the doll's negative influences.

The doll was placed in a room of the museum and various instruments were used to monitor it for any unusual activity. Strange disembodied sounds were captured before the full investigation even started. Voices came across a ghost box, and Annabelle seemed to be trying to influence Zak.

The SLS (Structured Light Sensor) camera, which maps energies attempting to manifest in humanoid form, captured a figure moving from the doll to Zak as if attempting to attach to him.

A controversy was created during this investigation that caused a real stir on social media. Zak touched the doll.

The incident unfolded slowly, with Zak asking Tony (who was in a different room monitoring the video feed) if he could hold Annabelle. Tony was adamant that Zak not touch the doll and a brief exchange took place with Zak repeatedly asking to be allowed to touch the doll.

During the course of the investigation, Zak reached out and touched Annabelle. Spera rapidly ended the investigation, packing Annabelle back in her case and leaving the premises.

After the special aired, a frenzy of comments broke out on social media, with people taking both sides of the fence about Zak touching the doll. There was in fact such a flurry from the incident that Zak released an official statement. Posted online on the Zak Bagans-Ghost Adventures Crew (GAC) Facebook page, the statement read:

November 4, 2017

"So many of you in outrage because I touched "Annabelle" so here's my response. While so many viewers think they know exactly what it's like to be in these type situations, in all due respect, they do not. I am a 100% sensitive.

What's that mean? I absorb and sense energies around me at a very high level. Whether it's from living people, residual energy, objects or from spirits. I've been like this my entire life. I am not a psychic medium. I am a sensitive. And while some perceive this to be "overreacting" or "too dramatic" well, those people will never be able to relate to what I feel when I'm around spirits. It's a rush, it's draining, it's exhilarating, it's terrifying all-in-one depending who or what I'm in contact with.

With that said, when it comes to "Annabelle," there was a tremendous amount of layered energy infusing this doll which I believe has caused a dark entity to use it to manipulate and influence the living. I also believe that it's past and present owners have put their energies into it as well...good and BAD. Its sat in an EXTREMELY HAUNTED AND CURSED occult museum for years, absorbing those other possessed artifact's energies as well while trapped in a glass case. All of this strengthening the entity(s) even more and more who use it as a host to manipulate the living.

Add the other layer to it. A doll that has made 100's of millions for movie studios, producers, etc. and with all that money comes greed, lawsuits, hate, etc. MORE negativity. Fueling the fire even more within that same very doll.

I was skeptical of "Annabelle" until she showed up and thru MULTIPLE pieces of our equipment documenting incredible evidence as well as myself, Billy and Aaron feeling extraordinary things DIRECTLY around and underneath it.

We received the clear spirit box voice "Annabelle" then "Anna" on Talking EVP. "Grab Leg" another command. The SLS evidence was amazing. Showing two figures inside of me when "Annabelle's" figure would leave her body. Then go into mine. There was too much to discount she was not legit.

During this event I became affected and I started feeling very sad for no reason. At which time we received "you" and "us" and this is when I feel whatever is in "Annabelle" was out and began to manipulate me. Many times I was near her. On the floor frigid cold and in a total trance, while Billy was sweating like he had a 104-degree fever, while Aaron was amazed at the communication she was doing thru multiple devices. What really disturbed Tony was him finally seeing hardcore evidence surrounding these events in person. As a witness.

I touched Annabelle but felt like I had to. Not because it would be a great TV moment but because of things most of you wouldn't understand... something had a grip on me and I had a tremendous amount of sadness thru the whole thing except one quick moment of rage near the end when Tony took her and left.

I'm sorry Tony and to Lorraine Warren for touching her but it was not my direct control in that moment. Touching her I feel has led to many strange events and I do believe was indeed a dangerous thing to do.

We had the honor to be the very first to investigate her on television and glad so many of you tuned in to witness it. Because we feel we accomplished an anticipated investigation resulting incredible evidence.

Tony Spera responded to the media attention too, clarifying the situation as best he could and offering his take on the incident. He stated clearly that he was not angry at Zak and the GAC crew and emphasized that he was concerned for everyone's safety:

"...I am not "mad" at Zak or the crew. Disappointed that Zak touched Annabelle—but not mad at him.

I was/am concerned for the safety of anyone who touches Annabelle."

Spera also clarified that he was given clear instructions by Ed Warren in the proper technique to pick up or touch the doll. Prior to the investigation, Spera took everyone though a protection technique taught to him by Warren that included asking for God's protection from anything evil, inhuman or demonic. Spera states that the crew were all blessed with holy water prior to dealing with Annabelle. Tony also states Zak and the crew were respectful during the filming:

"The entire crew and Zak were respectful—with the exception of when Zak became emotionally overwhelmed (probably the beginning of "obsession and oppression" and touched the doll). I didn't actually witness him touching her.

Afterwards, Zak and the crew were quite concerned about the consequences of Zak having touched the doll.

I will say that at one point in the investigation—Zak became confused and said he didn't feel right. He apparently was having a reaction to Annabelle being in the museum.

Tony writes that while he still believes Zak never should have touched Annabelle, he has considered that perhaps he himself never should have taken the doll to Las Vegas.

"Let's all just chill out and walk away with a renewed respect for the power of demonic forces."

The reason I agreed to do this was to show the audience that evil is real, that demons and Devils DO exist."

Mandy the Cracked Face Doll

Mandy the doll was donated to the Quesnel & District Museum in British Columbia, Canada in 1991. Little is known about Mandy's origins. She is a porcelain doll and historians have determined she was made in England or Germany between 1910 and 1920.

The doll was already over 90 years old when the museum received her. The museum's curator felt uneasy when she first took the doll. It was somewhat damaged and dirty, with a frayed and faded dress. Parts of the doll's body had rips and tears, a result of its age and perhaps the many children that had played with it over time. The truly unsettling thing however, was Mandy's face. The doll's forehead, just above the right eye, is cracked, causing the eye on that side to protrude slightly and making it appear that it's leering back at those who look at it.

The donor wished to remain anonymous, but she told the museum she could not handle having the doll in her home anymore. Why? Because very strange things happen around Mandy.

The woman reported that she would often wake up in the middle of the night to the sound of a child crying somewhere in her home. The sound would echo through the house and was so loud that it couldn't be ignored. The owner would investigate, but find nothing to explain the strange crying sounds. Oddly, each time, she would find a window in her basement open, the curtains blowing in the wind, but no sign of intruders. She was convinced the crying noise was connected to the old doll and, after she donated Mandy to the museum, she reported the crying in her home stopped.

But while the donor found peace, it wasn't long before curious things began to happen at the museum once they had Mandy. Staff members and volunteers at the Quesnel found that their lunches started disappearing out of the refrigerator, only to be found later tucked away in drawers. Other items also began to vanish; books, pictures, pencils, pens, and various office supplies, and even items that were part of museum displays. Some would reappear later, others have yet to be found. Unexplained footsteps started being heard around the museum at odd hours and when employees were alone.

When the doll was first received, it was put through the standard processes all new items at the museum receive. It was taken to a work room for some basic maintenance which began with it being sealed in a plastic bag. This was done to determine if there were any insects infesting the doll. Museum staff were even more uneasy around Mandy once she was placed in the bag however. Some workers said when they were in the room, they could hear the plastic bag rustling as if the doll wanted out. When they would walk over to check on Mandy, they would find her position in the bag had changed, as if she had indeed been moving around. No insects were found on the doll, so none of the staff could explain neither the movement nor the sounds.

The next part of the museum's process involved taking a series of photographs of the doll as part of the official record.

Experienced museum photographer Cookie Castle was in charge of taking photos of the newly acquired doll when it was added to the collection. Castle had a friend with her during the photo shoot and both reported they were extremely uncomfortable being alone with Mandy.

Castle was able to complete the photo session and head to the development room with her film. She developed the film and produced the negatives, hanging them up to dry. At that point, she and her friend cleaned up, locked all the doors and left the building.

The next day, museum curator Ruth Stubbs came in to find a disaster. She described the mess in the developing room as looking like *"A small child had a temper tantrum."*

Once the photographic documentation was completed, Mandy was left in the lab overnight. The next morning when the staff returned to work, they had quite the surprise. The room was in total disarray. Books, papers and small objects had been thrown wildly around the room and onto the floor. Larger, heavy objects had been pushed over. The lab had been completely trashed, but there were no signs of a break-in and nothing was stolen. In the midst of it all, there sat Mandy where she had been left by herself overnight.

Reports state that if Mandy is placed in a case with other dolls, things will be moved about and disrupted in the case and the other dolls will be knocked over. Shortly after being put on display, visitors started to complain the doll made them feel uneasy. A statement from the museum says Mandy was first put near the entrance:

"[Mandy]...sat facing the public entranceway, visitors would stare, and talk about this doll with the cracked and broken face and sinister smile. With time, Mandy was moved to another part of the museum and carefully placed in a case by herself because rumor had it that she should not be placed with the other dolls because she would harm them."

It wasn't long before word got out about Quesnel's haunted doll and people began to visit to see what all the fuss was about. Curiosity seekers started reporting their own odd experiences with Mandy, a portion of which include:

Batteries drain in her presence; electronic equipment is reported to malfunction, and cameras constantly act up. While some photos turn out completely normal, others come out blurry as if the doll was moving when the shot was taken, or unexplained light anomalies appear in the pictures.

One museum attendee from Calgary, Alberta, had difficulty trying to capture images of the haunted doll. Ruth Trussler, wanted to use her video camera and take some footage of Mandy. While she was filming, Ruth recalls thinking the doll did not like having her picture taken.

Ruth didn't have time to think about the random thought too closely however, since the indicator light on her video recorder started flashing intermittently.

Trussler moved through the museum and into the next exhibit where she discovered her video camera was working fine again.

Mandy the doll wasn't finished screwing with Ruth Trussler and her video camera however. When Ruth got home, she decided she would review the footage in her VCR. Popping the tape in, she found it jammed in her player and inoperable. The tape had to be forcibly removed and she was never able to review the footage she had taken at the Quesnel Museum.

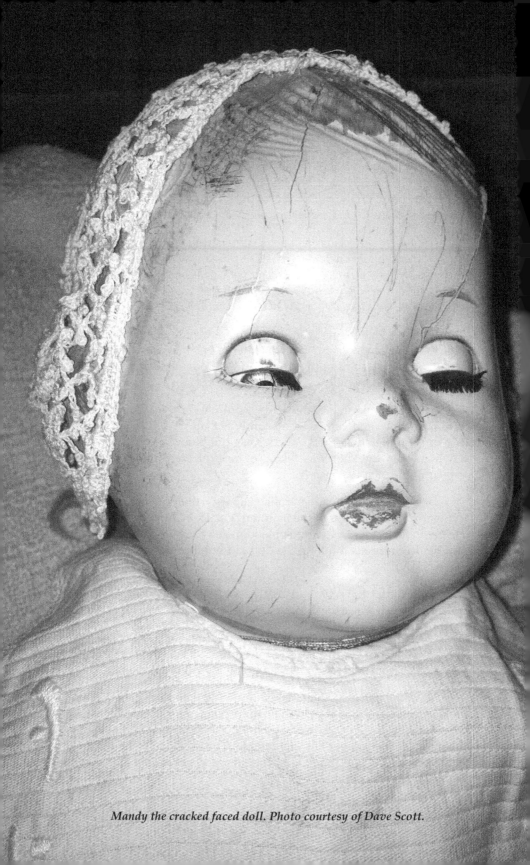

Mandy the cracked faced doll. Photo courtesy of Dave Scott.

Cariboo Observer photographer Ross Mitchell, had a difficult time during his experience taking photographs at the Quesnel museum. He took a wide range of photos of various exhibits and many of the shots were of the haunted doll. When Mitchell reached his office, he attempted to print contact sheets of his photos. But the paper never came out of his developer. Somewhere in the processing machine, the photos of Mandy had disappeared.

Mitchell sat about trying to resolve the problem. While examining the machine, he heard footsteps in the office area above the developing room. Ross was supposed to be completely alone in the building, so the sounds led him to believe there were intruders on the premises. Mitchell searched the building but could find no source for the anomalous sounds.

Mitchell wasn't the only news photographer who had strange experiences while attempting to photograph Mandy.

Quesnel Advocate photographer Seth Gotro visited the museum to take some shots of Mandy for a news piece. He too had odd experiences while attempting to capture photos of the doll. He later stated that although the doll was apparently an inanimate object, it appeared to *"turn her head away from the lens so that I might not get her on film."*

Gotro was determined to get the job finished and obtained the photos he needed so he removed the doll from its glass case in order to get clear and unobstructed photographs. He still found the doll unsettling, reporting on the experience he stated:

"She seemed to be grinning at me as the flash hit her face."

Countless people report changes in Mandy's facial expression and have said they felt Mandy's eyes follow them as they moved around the room. Some even claim they see Mandy blink her eyes.

A folktale surrounding the doll claims to tell the tale of the spirit inhabiting the antique:

Purportedly, the doll was originally found in the cellar of an old farmhouse. According to the legend, a man was walking by the place when he heard someone crying from inside. This was odd since the farmhouse had been long abandoned. The man approached the home and knocked at the door, but there was no answer. Still, the crying continued, so he entered the home thinking perhaps someone was

93

in trouble. Once inside, he realized the crying was coming from the cellar, so he went back outside and found the entrance. Making his way into the cellar, the man made a disturbing discovery. The body of a young girl, long dead, was on the floor. In her arms, was the doll now known as Mandy.

It's unknown how the little girl came to be in the cellar, but some believe it is her spirit that has taken up residence in the creepy little doll with the cracked face that now sits in the Quesnel museum.

The Haunting of Harold the Doll

"I wouldn't say it's either haunted, or cursed. I wouldn't say it's "possessed" either. What it is goes far beyond all three of those. It's not like anything I've ever read, or heard about in paranormal literature."

Anthony Quinata, owner of Harold the doll.

Harold's story is one of the most curious of haunted doll tales. He is twenty-one inches in height and appears to have been manufactured in the 1930's. It's a composition doll, with the head, arms and legs all made from composite particles, water and plaster. The dolls eyes close when it is laying down.

Harold made his debut on eBay in 2004. By most accounts, He was the first purportedly haunted doll that went up for auction on the popular site. The original seller, Greg Mishka, posted details about the strange doll claiming he found it at a flea market. As Mishka relates, it was late in the day and most of the dealers were packing up to head home. He saw an elderly man packing the doll in a box and asked if he could see the item. The seller acted odd, not wanting to show Mishka the doll at first. Mishka proceeded to ask the man how much he wanted for the doll. The man responded:

"Well, that's a good question, because it's very old... (the man looked like he was going to begin to cry) ...it was my son's, I bought it for him when he was born, and he passed away a few years after...this doll has sat in my work shed for over 60 years. I wasn't going to bring it out today, but I figured I just needed to get it out of there...anyways, I want 20 bucks for it."

Mishka paid the man, put the doll in a bag, and walked away. As he made his way out of the flea market, the seller came running after him, visibly out of breath, he told Mishka:

"I have to warn you about something, I can't just let you take him like this…the reason it has been in my shed, is that the doll brought an eerie presence into our house after our son died…we could hear crying and singing from his bedroom…when we went to check it out, there was nothing, just the doll."

The old man told Mishka that other manifestations began to happen in the home. Out of concern, the man contacted a priest who told him to burn the doll to be rid of the negative energy. The man attempted to burn the doll but had no success. The doll, he claimed, would not burn. He stated that the wear on the figure's arms and legs were from his attempts to light the doll on fire.

Mishka later wrote that he was amused by the story, but brushed it off. However once he got home, disturbing things started to happen in his life. A week after bringing the doll home he began to hear children laughing and crying in the basement where he kept Harold. It was the least of his problems. His cat died, his girlfriend left him to run off with a pool tech, and he developed chronic migraines.

Of course, when he investigated the basement, he could find nothing to explain the sounds. Mishka became convinced the doll was haunted by some evil presence and decided to sell it on eBay.

Labeling it as a "cursed doll," the listing stated it had been stored in an armadillo coffin in Mishka's basement for a year and a half and he "needed to get rid of it."

"I really do believe it's cursed, sometimes I touch it, and it seems like it has a pulse, maybe I'm just paranoid, maybe not."

The purportedly haunted doll was a big hit on the auction site, and by the time bidding closed, Harold had sold for almost seven hundred dollars. The winner however, couldn't pay, and Harold went back on the market. The doll later sold and was out of Greg Mishka's hands and off to its new owner.

The successful auction inspired other dealers to jump into the market to sell haunted dolls. They carved out their own niche on eBay and other auction sites that continue to thrive today.

The story of Harold the doll was fascinating, but another twist in the tale came five years after its initial listing when Mishka revealed the truth. He had made up the entire story. Harold, he said, was not really haunted. The revelation came in 2009 when Mishka published an article online stating he had fabricated the tale of Harold's origin and the reports of paranormal activity as a gimmick to sell the doll for a higher price at auction.

Between the revelations, and the time Mishka sold the doll however, Harold's new owner reported that she was experiencing disturbing incidents due to her ownership of the doll. Her Aunt reportedly made fun of the doll and immediately afterwards, the woman's back when out with a herniated disc. Oddly, the owner herself also soon suffered a herniated disc, as did the aunt's fiancé.

Other more serious incidents occurred in the woman's life while she owned Harold. A friend of hers laughed at the doll, commenting on the bad shape it was in. A few days later, she fell down a flight of steps and suffered a fractured skull and brain injuries. She died as a result of the accident.

Another man, who stayed in the same room as the doll, suddenly developed stage four cancer and was given a short time to live. All after he had received a previous clean bill of health.

The woman soon decided to rid herself of the doll, and Harold was again up for auction. It was sold in 2004 to a gentleman named Anthony Quinata making him the third owner of Harold. Quinata experienced paranormal activity around the doll and put it in storage where it primarily remained from 2005-2013.

Quinata is from Guam, an island near the Philippines and Japan. His aunt was Japanese and was one of the inspirations that led him to delve into the paranormal:

"My interest in the paranormal began when I was 7 years old, listening to my Aunt Sue, who was Japanese, telling me ghost stories and folk tales from Japan...which led me to becoming a paranormal investigator beginning in 1989, specializing in investigating haunts, apparitions and poltergeist activity until 2006."

Quinata kept the doll out of the public eye for nine years, bringing it out of storage after he realized there was still a big interest in haunted dolls. In short order, Harold was in the spotlight. Despite the fact Mishka had recanted his story of the doll's haunted nature, it seemed there was indeed something supernatural about it. Quinata began to collect and record evidence from his dealings with Harold.

There are a great number of misconceptions about Harold. Most of the common knowledge about the doll came from the original listing, and later revelations made by the original seller, Greg Mishka. Quinata later learned the man had originally found Harold in his brother's apartment in New York. He believed his brother had purchased the doll at an antique store or indoor flea market in Brooklyn, a partial inspiration for the fabricated story on the original eBay listing.

When Quinata first won the doll, he asked April, a friend of his, to do a psychic reading on it. The reading lasted only moments before April started trembling and crying.

"I'm sorry Anthony, but I can't do this."

"Why not?" he asked.

"He just told me he's going to kill me!"

Anthony told her it was okay and packed the doll away as April explained further:

"I'm really sorry, but I have a heart murmur, and I heard Harold say, 'I'm going to kill you.' Then it started to feel as though he was grabbing my heart."

When Quinata got home, he reviewed the digital recording he'd made of the brief session. He was shocked to hear several EVPs that were captured by the recorder while April was talking. The first was an angry male voice that said, "Shut up!" The second was an agonizing scream. Most disturbing however, was the third EVP, a male voice shouting:

"I'm going to kill you, bitch!"

To date, four psychics have done readings on Harold in an attempt to divine more information about the origins of the doll. After each reading, the psychic refused to have anything more to do with the doll.

Numerous people reported negative experiences they attributed to Harold. Some were affected simply by reading internet postings about the doll, others reported affects after watching videos featuring Harold.

One woman wrote to tell Anthony that her mother became physically ill and started vomiting blood after they laughed about the doll.

Several people have witnessed the doll's eyes turn from blue to charcoal black.

Other reports of effects from the doll include headaches, migraines, back pain and unexplained injuries.

"I've heard from numerous people who became ill, or had a string of bad luck happen after simply looking at a picture of the doll. And then of course, there are those people who have mocked the doll, or watched videos, read my blog posts, etc….and nothing happens to them. And I'm convinced that there are those people who do provoke it, and something does happen, but they sure as hell aren't going to admit it for fear of it happening again."

EVP sessions done around the doll have picked up numerous voices accompanied by screaming and laughter.

Quinata believes Harold is neither haunted, possessed, or cursed; rather, he believes, numerous entities use the doll as a vessel. He writes that there are five spirits involved with the doll, four human and one non-human entity. He believes he knows the non-human entity's name and it's identified in the bible as a "prince of hell."

Quinata has had intense experiences as a result of owning the doll. He says a friend of his passed away as a result of the haunted object. He dedicated his book on Harold to:

"My friend, Tereva, and to my fur baby, Chance. Both of whom are victims in my war with the doll. I'm so sorry, I miss you both beyond words."

Quinata's experiences have brought him close to getting rid of the doll on occasion, especially after the death of his beloved puppy Chance:

"…one of the entities in the doll killed one of my puppies. Chance had a herniated diaphragm, and his abdominal organs were in his chest. Two veterinarians couldn't explain how it happened, as he didn't have any fractured or broken bones to suggest he was hit by a car."

Quinata states that after the dog's death, he was still unsure whether one of the entities was definitely responsible. Then a swarm of flies showed up in the house he was staying in at the time. A video further confirmed the supernatural influence:

"I was filming a vlog showing the flies (which can be seen on my YouTube channel) and in the attic window of the house next door, you can see that reflection of several apparitions including one with horns coming out of

his head. I knew then that the entity was rubbing it in my face."

The next day, while mourning the loss of his dog, Quinata thought briefly about getting rid of the cursed doll, afraid of losing his other dog. He quickly dismissed the idea, and instead became angry at the level of negative energy being projected at him by what he believed inhabited the doll. He resolved to continue on his course and publish a book containing all the information he had uncovered about Harold.

The doll being back in the public eye brought another level of attention to haunted Harold, and it wasn't long before TV called on Anthony with an interesting request. Paranormal reality show Ghost Adventures wanted to take Harold with them to the infamous Island of the Dolls in Mexico. Quinata agreed and Harold ended up on what many count as one of the show's best episodes.

The aftermath of the show had many affects. Quinata posted an account on his blog about an encounter he had on a plane in October 2015:

"I was on a plane, sitting next to a guy who was watching Ghost Adventures on his computer. It happened to be the Island of the Dolls episode."

Quinata struck up a conversation and asked the man if he was a fan of the show. The man replied he wasn't really, but thought it might be interesting to watch, so he was giving it a try. It was then that Harold appeared on the screen.

"I have that doll," he told the man.

The man was clearly skeptical of Quinata's claim.

"Seriously," Quinata replied, telling the man the story of the eBay auction.

"Watch the show…if you have any questions, I'll be happy to answer them for you."

After the man finished the show, he looked at Quinata and asked:

"Where is the doll now?"

"In the overhead compartment right above us," Quinata replied.

The response clearly unsettled Quinata's fellow passenger.

"The blood left his face, and I thought he was going to pass out! He

never said a word to me after that."

Quinata believes the spirits that reside within the doll target him as well as those close to him. There's not always a rhyme or reason to who suffers attacks either. A friend of Anthony's, Camille, has been attacked numerous times by the forces in the doll. Although she has always been respectful towards Harold, it is clear something attached to the doll dislikes her. Quinata himself deals with countless attacks and acknowledges:

"I not only feel unsafe, I know I'm not safe. I'm under constant attack from it."

Why keep such a negative item? For Quinata it's personal, as he believes it has fallen on him to free the innocent spirits within Harold:

"...it's fallen on me to figure out some way to release them. 'Trapped' isn't a good word...they are being held prisoner, by one of the entities. That's what makes this case so different from the typical "haunted doll" story."

Harold is a true puzzle of the paranormal. Is he really haunted? Possessed? Cursed? Perhaps the years of attention focused on the doll have imbued it with energy, causing it to exude its own limited consciousness. Or perhaps like many other haunted objects, there are multiple reasons it has become instilled with something unearthly.

Either way it appears the story of haunted Harold is far from over.

Peggy the Doll

"That doll nearly ruined my life, I want to forget it ever existed and I hope God protects you all."

JW—Original owner of Peggy the Doll.

Imagine a doll so haunted, so powerful, that viewing photos or videos of it online can lead to nausea, crippling headaches, chest pains and even heart attacks.

Meet Peggy.

Peggy is of unknown age. She's a large doll, about three feet tall. She wears a white dress and has blonde hair. She currently resides at Zak Bagans' Haunted Museum in Las Vegas, Nevada. Her story however, began in the UK.

Paranormal investigator Jayne Harris, head of HD Paranormal, and a specialist in haunted dolls, was first contacted by the doll's owner in the fall of 2014 via an email that contained a desperate plea for help. In part, the email stated:

"I can't talk to anyone about this, as I am sure they will think I am crazy. Some days I wonder if I'm crazy myself. I have a doll here which I am sure is causing my house, maybe even me, to be haunted. If I hadn't lived through it for the last few months, I'd think that sounded completely insane. "

"JW," Peggy's previous owner, reported a series of disturbing incidents to HD paranormal. According to Harris, the woman would wake up, hot and shaken, after horrible nightmares. No matter where she moved the doll in her home, the terrible dreams continued. She called in a local priest to bless her home, but after two separate visits, there was no improvement. In fact, things got even worse in JW's home. As the night terrors continued, the woman became very ill with a high fever. She even started to suffer from hallucinations. Fortunately she recovered, but enough was enough. She searched online for resources on the topic of haunted dolls, looking for an answer and a way to deal with the doll. She came across Harris and her group and contacted the investigator immediately.

Harris took the doll to her home base in Shrewsbury, Shropshire. She put the doll in the basement of her home where she's kept other haunted objects, and proceeded to investigate the activity around it.

It wasn't long before Jayne herself began to suffer ill effects, seemingly from the presence of the doll. Six weeks after Peggy was in her home, a strange illness set in on Jayne. As she states:

"I began to suffer with incredibly debilitating fatigue, to the point at which after 2 weeks of migraines, nausea and dizziness, I was unable to get out of bed, and if I did make it down the stairs, I made it no further than the sofa."

Blood tests came back normal and three independent doctors could give no explanation to Jayne to explain what was happening to her.

Harris was skeptical that the doll could be the source of her

101

illness. As a trained mental health specialist, she tries to take a logical approach when dealing with unusual phenomena. However, all signs continually pointed to the presence of the doll. She was finally convinced to have it taken out of the house for a time. Four days later, Jayne started to feel normal again. It seemed there was much more to Peggy than the investigator first believed, and the doll led her to question many things. As she recalls:

"The introduction of the doll we now call Peggy would lead me to question not only the untapped abilities of the human mind, but also the reality of existence as we perceive it, and the intricate layers that our souls may weave through on the journey to their ultimate resting place."

There were more strange revelations to come. Continuing her investigation of the haunted doll, Harris and her team started posting photos of Peggy online. Right away, it was clear the doll's reach was extensive. Reports began to flood Harris's inbox. Countless people described strange phenomena and reactions as a result of simply viewing photos of Peggy the doll on their computers.

One woman claimed her computer froze on a picture of Peggy and the room turned ice cold. According to Harris:

"She then said she felt someone in the room with her and could hear them moving around. This lady was messaging me at the time via Facebook, asking me to quickly advise her on what to do."

Another witness reported that light bulbs in her home started blowing when she began to talk about Peggy. Other reports were of overwhelming anxiety and strange visions of mental institutions and abuse. Reports of migraines, heart palpitations, shortness of breath, the list went on and on. One writer told Harris that looking at the doll online caused her asthma to flare up. The more known Peggy became, the more reports there were.

But the consequences of Peggy's online presence didn't end there. When Harris posted a video of the haunted doll, a whole new range of reports rolled in from people suffering after viewing it. A British woman claimed she had a heart attack after watching the video. (The notorious video clip that purportedly caused the heart attack remains online for those brave enough to view it. It's posted with a warning to "watch at your own risk.") Harris says she never had a case so intense.

Not much is known about the true history of Peggy. JW, the original owner, had little to add to the story. In fact, as soon as she was rid of the doll, she wanted nothing more to do with it. Harris and her team spent time trying to gather both physical evidence of paranormal activity, as well as employing various psychic techniques in an attempt to learn more about the doll and its troubled behavior. Harris notes that a crucifix was placed around the doll's neck and Peggy seemed to have an aversion to it.

Two different mediums told the team they believed the spirit inhabiting Peggy was Jewish and has a link to the holocaust. Curiously, automatic writing sessions done in Peggy's presence have brought forth the word "star" as well as the name "David," possibly implying a link to the Jewish Star of David.

Other researchers believe the spirit connected to the doll is that of a woman born in London in 1946, who later died of a chest related condition, possibly asthma. It's another curious connection considering that many people report chest pains after viewing Peggy.

Whatever the true history, each medium who reads the doll picks up a consistent feeling; that the entity is restless, frustrated, and suffered much persecution in life. Harris and others believe the spirit in the doll actively tries to prevent extensive information from getting out.

"Just the other night we held a session with her and I made lots of notes as the pendulum was going crazy. The next morning, I couldn't find my notepad anywhere, and when I did find it, I couldn't even reach it. It had been placed up in the joists of the ceiling in our basement. My husband had to use a ladder to get it. Many people who saw the picture felt that she did not want me to tell people the information I had gained."

There are also numerous stories claiming Peggy shows up in people's dreams. One woman reported to Harris the doll had appeared to her in a dream, issuing a warning about one of the woman's cats. The next morning, she awoke to find her cat very ill. The animal died the next day.

A medium known as "Lindy," had a unique set of experiences that she connected to Peggy when she posted her impressions about the doll online:

"When I commented my thoughts and feelings, all my comments were duplicated—no one else's, just mine. I tried commenting on other threads and nothing happened, but as soon as I went back to that one, the same thing happened. My dog started barking and my face became very hot and flushed.

I felt like I wasn't alone. I ended up apologizing to Peggy as I felt maybe she disproved of us chatting about her and my symptoms stopped."

Lindy's connection with Peggy did have some positive consequences. After watching a video about Peggy, something pushed Lindy to have a long overdue conversation with her daughter about the girl's mental health issues:

"My daughter has been unwell for months and things were strained and stressful. Late that morning, I found myself having a much-needed heart-to-heart with her. All the things I had wanted to say for months were just flowing from my mouth. I've found it very difficult communicating in such a way with her due to her illness. I felt that Peggy had helped me."

Lindy had no idea an automatic writing session with Peggy was taking place at the same time as her conversation with her daughter. When she went online, she saw images of the session and the messages that had been received. Among them was one that seemed to be directed at her:

"The words 'Lindy girl explanation draw a line' were written on the paper. I couldn't believe my eyes. It was basically what had just been talked about between me and my daughter."

Harris continued receiving emails from people being tormented after viewing the haunted doll. Each time, she would take the doll into an isolation area and ask it to stop attacking the person. Usually the tactic worked.

Numerous psychics offered to clear the doll of its negative attachments, or to take the doll themselves, but each time, Harris refused. Instead she and her team continued to conduct various experiments, gathering evidence of the chaos created by Peggy. She emphasizes:

"In order to do the work I do well, I have to approach each case as a skeptic initially and look for 'normal' explanations for things. If it were one or two occasions that things were happening on, I could do that, but with Peggy I just know there's something more."

One of the curious aspects of accounts involving Peggy is the reported reactions of animals, especially dogs. While it's commonly known that animals are more sensitive to paranormal activity and perceive it at a different level, it's unusual for such reactions to come from an online connection. Numerous people reported their dogs behaving strangely when images or videos of the doll were on display. For example, F. Lead wrote Jayne with this account:

"NEW DOLL OMG! — Guys, I opened her photo and my dog started going crazy! Spinning in circles barking. I switched it off, he stopped, switched it on he started again! Now he's hiding and trembling. WTF!" F. Lead.

Jayne reports that around eighty percent of the people who have any kind of contact with the doll, including online, experience some kind of negative reaction. It's a troubling component of the paranormal qualities of the doll:

"Possibly the most worrying aspect of this case centers around the apparent ability this spirit (or energy) has to bring about physical, recordable reactions and effects in certain people. Of course, to a degree we can put some instances down to suggestion, especially given that Peggy now has a degree of notoriety."

In April 2015, Jayne was contacted by a US based production company working on a new television show. They asked if she would be willing to transport Peggy to Las Vegas, Nevada to appear on "Deadly Possessions," a show hosted by Zak Bagans with a spotlight on haunted objects.

Harris eventually agreed to do the show, and by the end of 2015, she and her husband were on their way to the United States. Not wanting to carry the large doll on the flight with them for various reasons, they carefully packed Peggy and shipped her to Vegas.

Strange things even happened during the filming of the show. Harris recalls that an unexplainable swarm of flies made the interview difficult:

"One of the strange things to happen while Zak and I were speaking on film was that we seemed to be being bombarded by flies as soon as Zak began suggesting that Peggy may not like attention. It was very sudden, and they were really invasive, constantly landing on our faces while we were trying to speak, Zak more so."

No one working on the production could find an explanation for the sudden swarm of flies, nor had they ever experienced anything like it before. It was both distracting and rather concerning.

"Zak made reference to the fact that it is common in cases of demonic presence to get these infestations, which didn't make me feel very comfortable

as you can imagine! We took a break as the flies were getting too intense and affecting the filming."

The filming complete, Jayne and her husband, and Peggy, returned to the UK. Once the episode of Deadly Possessions aired, even more attention was put on Peggy. The show was well received, and Harris continued her research on the doll and its possible origins.

In early 2017, Zak contacted Jayne via email, just checking in on the surface, but Harris knew exactly why he was reaching out. She'd already been told via a psychic that the time was coming to let go of Peggy and let the doll and its spirit take the next step in its journey.

Zak had been hard at work building his collection of haunted items for a museum in Las Vegas. Once they spoke on the phone, Jayne learned Zak was indeed interested in purchasing Peggy to add to the collection.

Although Jayne asked for time to think it over, she knew the decision was already made. In short order, Peggy was on her way once again to Nevada, this time to take up her new permanent residence at Zak's museum.

Zak placed the doll in her own room in the mansion. The same room that had been used for a séance during a special episode of Ghost Adventures.

At the completion of her time with the haunted doll, Jayne Harris wrote a book detailing all the strange incidents that occurred while Peggy was in her possession. Titled "Peggy the Doll: a very different haunting," It's an excellent read and one of the few books to fully chronicle a specific haunted doll.

While attending the grand opening event for the museum, I had the opportunity to see Peggy myself.

The doll's room is one of the "challenges" visitors are presented with during the tour. Essentially, several of the more notorious objects in the museum are presented in such a way that visitors have a choice whether or not to view the object. Standing in front of the door to the doll's room, the tour guide briefly explains the notoriety of Peggy and the intense possibilities that may result from being in her presence. The choice of whether to enter the room is left to each person individually. Those who do choose to enter are encouraged to be nice and greet Peggy. Looking directly at Peggy may lead to serious problems, so even if one enters the room, another choice must be made when it comes to looking directly at the doll.

The museum of course, takes no responsibility for any ill effects resulting from being in the doll's presence. Interestingly, hardly anyone in the tour group I was with that day chose to enter the room, rather they waited outside for the next portion of the tour. Peggy, it seemed, was considered the most dangerous object in a museum filled with creepy items from around the world.

At one point in an exchange on social media site Twitter, a fan asked Zak what item from Deadly Possessions had affected him the most. His response:

"As crazy as it sounds, Peggy."

Home of Peggy. Photo by author.

Okiku the Living Doll

Japan, 1918. Seventeen-year-old Eikichi Suzuki is visiting Sapporo, on the island of Hokkaido for a marine exhibition. Walking on Tanuki-koji, Sapporo's famous shopping street, Eikichi decides to purchase a special doll for his two-year-old sister, Okiku.

The doll is about sixteen inches tall, and is dressed in a traditional Japanese kimono. The life-like porcelain white face is set with black beads for eyes, and the doll's coal black hair is cut at shoulder length. The family is not wealthy, and Eikichi does all he can to take care of his little sister. When he presented her the doll, it was just as he had hoped, she was overjoyed with the gift. From the time she received it, the girl kept the doll with her constantly. She even named the doll after herself, dubbing it, too, Okiku.

For a year, the little girl and her special doll were constant companions, then, a terrible tragedy befell young Okiku. She contracted influenza and complications from the virus lead to her untimely death.

The devastated family went into a period of mourning and placed their daughter's beloved doll on the family altar, the location where they said their daily prayers, including prayers for their deceased child.

Soon, the family began to notice something very strange. The doll Okiku was changing. Its hair, which had originally been at shoulder length. was getting longer. While the hair had been straight and even when it was in their daughter's possession, now, the hair became uneven with some strands growing longer than others. How was such a thing possible? Puzzled, the family continued to keep track of the apparent growth of hair on the inanimate object.

It wasn't long before the doll Okiku's hair had grown all the way down to its knees. The family tried trimming the doll's hair, but it soon grew back. Again, the doll's hair grew all the way to its knees. At this point, the family came to the conclusion that their daughter's spirit was restless and had taken up residency in the porcelain doll. It was the presence of her spirit, they believed, that was causing the doll's hair to grow. A sign for them perhaps, or simply a side effect of the spirit's attachment.

In 1938, the family decided to relocate to Sakhalin. Preparing for their relocation, they were afraid to move the doll to their new home, but because of the spirit they believed to be attached to it, they were also unwilling to dispose of the doll. They took the doll to the Mannenji Temple in Iwamizawa, Hokkaido, Japan. Meeting with the temple's elder priest, the family explained the strange qualities of the doll and expressed their belief that their daughter's spirit was trapped within. They asked the priest if the temple would take the doll and care for it and the earth-bound spirit attached to it.

The priest agreed, and the temple accepted the doll into their care.

Curiously, the name Okiku is also connected to one of Japan's most famous ghostly legends. It's the story of an unfortunate servant and her death and afterlife as a vengeful spirit.

The tale of Okiku the maid has been portrayed in numerous novels and a renowned Kabuki play. The story tells the tale of a young servant girl named Okiku, who works at the mansion of the samurai Tessan Aoyama. The samurai master becomes infatuated with the maid and tries to seduce her, but she rejects him. Angered, the man comes up with a devious plot to make her submit. He hides one of ten valuable Dutch plates and threatens Okiku that he will publicly announce she stole the plate unless she becomes his mistress. In despair, the young maid throws herself into a well and dies in the water below. After her death, Okiku's spirit returns each night, appearing before Aoyama and counting out from one to nine, then breaking into a terrible howl and sobbing. Tormented by the constant visits of the spirit, the samurai goes insane.

There are several variations of the Okiku ghost story to be found in Japan. One version of the tale involves a plot against a feudal lord which the servant girl overheard and reported. In this version she is killed out of revenge and her body thrown in a well. One tourist attraction at Himeji Castle, a hilltop complex in Himeji, Hyogo, is "Okiku's well," the supposed location of the young girl's death.

There are other such locations in Japan, indicating the story of Okiku likely has some grains of truth but the actual details have been obscured in the fog of history. Did the ghostly tale of Okiku the maid influence the story of the doll with growing hair? While the stories do not seem to be connected other than by the girl's name, folklorists find such connections intriguing, and there's always the potential the story of the doll was somehow inspired by the previous tale of a restless spirit named Okiku. At the least, it's curious that Japanese folklore now has two strange stories involving girls named Okiku.

Like the spirit of the maid, the haunted Okiku doll has become well known in Japan and has found its way into popular culture including films and novels.

To this day, the doll Okiku remains in the care of the temple, located on the outskirts of town. The temple's priests have long observed the regular growth of Okiku's hair and trimming it has become a regular duty at the temple.

Around the temple, there are numerous photos showing Okiku with varying lengths of hair. The doll rests quietly in a simple wooden box and no matter how often its hair is trimmed, it continues to grow back.

To date, no one has been able to explain why the doll's hair continues to grow. Samples of the hair have been scientifically analyzed and it has been verified that the hair is human.

Okiku remains at the Mannenji temple, still dressed in its traditional kimono, its coal black eyes gaze out at its surroundings. The temple's priests quietly carry out their regular duties, including the trimming of the doll's hair when it becomes necessary. According to some recent reports, authorities at the Mannenji Temple have moved the doll to a more private area of the complex and it is no longer available for public viewing.

Claire

In their book, "Haunted Objects," Christopher Balzano and Tim Weisberg recount the story of "Claire," a haunted doll owned by Jill Cole.

Claire was a gift given to Jill when she was only eight years old. The porcelain doll was a present from family friend "Miss Marian."

Jill wasn't a child who played with dolls much, but she placed Claire in a child sized rocking chair beside her nightlight, a place of honor, since it was a gift from the elderly woman Jill thought so much of.

It turned out to be the last gift Jill received from Miss Marian, as the old woman passed away shortly after bringing Jill the doll.

Jill recalls that "frightening things began to happen" in short order after the doll was brought to the house:

"I was always uneasy with Claire."

"I never wanted to touch her, and when I played in my room, it was as if she was watching me. It wasn't anything to panic about, but I do remember feeling like if I did something wrong, she might actually tell on me. How ridiculous does that sound?"

Activity was minor at first but soon escalated. Jill began to wake with a woman, inches from her face, shouting her name.

Items began to vanish, only to be found later, laying in front of the doll. The doll itself seemed to grow more active. The terror culminated for Jill the night she awoke to a thumping sound in her room. Looking towards the source, the corner of her room where the doll Clair sat, Jill witnessed something that haunts her to this day. As the authors recount:

"Staring at the doll, Jill saw its feet, which had previously been pointed in opposite directions, slowly straighten themselves until they were both pointing up. In a moment of horror that still haunts Jill's nightmares to this day, the doll turned its head toward Jill."

At that moment, Jill reports four music boxes in her room all began to play. The girl screamed out and the music stopped.

Jill packed the doll away and tried to forget about the incidents. It was years later, as an adult, that Jill shared the story of the haunted doll. Tim Weisberg was able to convince the woman to let him borrow the doll, so he could run some tests and attempt to document paranormal activity around the item. He ran EVP sessions to no avail and also checked for EMF readings with few results.

However, on the first night he had the doll, he took it to the studio while he recorded a show and reports a strange incident. As he states in his book and on his show Spooky Southcoast:

"...during the show, we experienced strange double-exposures of our video while it was recording, something that had never occurred before. It only happened on one of the three cameras we used, and I couldn't duplicate it again after the show was finished."

Weisberg also reports he heard a conversation coming from his office where the doll was kept:

"It sounded like two distinct voices, male and female. When I got to the office, they stopped talking."

In an appearance on Spooky Southcoast, Jill reports that even transporting the doll to the post office was a creepy experience. Driving with the doll in the trunk of her car, she heard a female voice. There was no radio on and she first thought it was her phone, but she verified it was not. There was no explanation for the source of the voice.

Weisberg documented some other incidents involving the doll, including something meddling with the temperature controls in his home, and a strange scratching sound that manifested in the house.

Jill also reports that Miss Marian had strange experiences with the doll, apparently it would move about the home on its own. Perhaps the strangest aspect of the story of Claire is that Miss Marian had no knowledge of where the doll came from. She found it one day while cleaning out a closet and had no recall of buying it or of it being given to her.

It should also be noted, Miss Marian believed her house was haunted by the victims of a tragic train wreck that occurred less than a mile away from her property. The accident took place in 1900 when a train plunged into a swollen creek and thirty-eight people lost their lives.

Today, Jill has no fear of Claire the haunted doll. In fact, she reflects on her experiences in a positive manner:

"Claire will always be both a special and terrifying memory from my childhood. She's the reason I believe what I believe when it comes to spirituality and it's helped shape my religious beliefs. She's one reason I delve into the paranormal as much as I do. I want answers for why she is what she is."

Claire is currently kept by a friend of Jill's in a haunted Victorian house in Atlanta, Georgia. The man is a Houngan, a Voodoo priest, and he keeps the spirit of the doll at peace and in check along with the other spirits that fill his home.

Mr. Creepy Seeks Mrs. Creepy

Nestled in the heart of downtown Seattle, a flight of steps leads to a surviving portion of the city's famous underground. A sign at street level reads: "Spooked in Seattle," and for those interested in ghost & hauntings, the paranormal, and the city's history, the site is a treasure trove.

Spooked in Seattle is headquarters for the city's leading ghost tour company, as well as the home of Seattle's "Death Museum." The business is also home to one of the most unsettling haunted ventriloquist dolls that has surfaced in recent history.

The doll's previous owner, the operator of an antique store in Washington state, dubbed the figure "Mr. Creepy." Purportedly, the "creepiness" of the doll could be felt on a daily basis while it was in the store. The handmade figure sat for many years on the bottom shelf of a display case in the shop. It was clear many customers found the doll unsettling, and most shoppers would ignore it or rush by in order to escape its strange gaze.

It should come as no surprise that the origins of the doll are unusual and unique. In fact, the story of Mr. Creepy is a somewhat sad one. Sometime in the 1960s, an elderly, and mostly forgotten, ventriloquist artist from the Vaudeville period was spending his retirement years making custom dolls. He occasionally displayed his well-honed ventriloquist talents at local events, showing off his hand made dolls and throwing his voice to bring them to life. In time however, he grew too weak to continue and retired from any performing.

In his twilight years, the artist made two very special dolls, one in his own likeness, and one in the likeness of his beloved wife. Carefully crafted by his own hands, the artist made the dolls as a representation of the couple's undying love. To make the figures even more realistic, the man used he and his wife's real hair, he wanted the dolls to be as much a part of them as possible, a strange replacement for the children the couple had never had. Perhaps he was trying to instill some portion of he and his wife's spirit, so their connection would be forever on display. During the couple's remaining years, the dolls never spent a day apart, just like the husband and wife they were modeled after.

Sadly, in the late 1970s, a tragic accident took the lives of the

Mr. Creepy & Friends. Photo by author.

couple. After their passing, their possessions were sold, including the beloved handmade, ventriloquist dolls. The dolls were sold as a pair, and through the years, they changed hands numerous times, continuing to be sold as a couple. It was sometime in 2013 that Mr. Creepy became separated from his female counterpart.

It's believed the female doll was somehow misplaced during the shuffle of moving inventory. The antique dealer has numerous storage locations, so the female doll may have ended up in a warehouse, or perhaps she's still packed away in some of the antique store's inventory, hidden from view in a mass of vintage items.

The separation may have been the impetus for Mr. Creepy's paranormal activity, since it was shortly after the separation of the two dolls that the store owner began to notice strange activity from Mr. Creepy. Reportedly, there began to be slight movements of the ventriloquist doll's head. One day, Mr. Creepy would be looking to his left, the next day, his head would be turned, and he would be looking to the right. The doll was secure in its display case, so no one was accessing it or moving it about. On some mornings, the shop owner would arrive at his store to find the doors to Mr. Creepy's case sitting wide open. Was the doll roaming the store at night in search of his missing mate?

Enter Ross Allison, well known ghost hunter and head of Spooked in Seattle, who came across Mr. Creepy and the strange tale connected to him while visiting the antique store. When he asked the owner if he would be willing to part with Mr. Creepy, there was not a moment's hesitation and the odd ventriloquist doll was off to his new residence at Spooked in Seattle, a welcome part of the haunted doll collection held by the museum.

Mr. Creepy was placed on display in a protective glass case in a public area of Spooked in Seattle.

Not long after Mr. Creepy had been transported to his new home, another one of Spooked in Seattle's owners heard a loud bang on one of the glass cases in the main area. Inspecting the display area, the man found Mr. Creepy leaning his head forward against the glass case. Surprised by his discovery, the man took a picture of the doll in its new placement. A later review of the photo revealed a strange anomaly, what appears to be a lifelike face of a man instead of the doll's face. Was the spirit of Mr. Creepy becoming more active?

With his most recent move to Seattle, it seems Mr. Creepy is still looking for his lost companion. Many of the staff members at Spooked in Seattle have witnessed him turning his head from time to time and changing his position in the display case in which he is kept. While there are other purportedly haunted items at the location, none seem to be as unusual as the strange ventriloquist doll. Apparently, the restless spirit attached to the doll is still looking for his bride.

Allison says that the antique store owner remains on the lookout for the elusive "Mrs. Creepy." Perhaps at some point she'll be found, and the dolls can be reunited. Will it quell the spirt? Perhaps someday Allison and the Spooked in Seattle staff will have a chance to see what happens when the two dolls are brought back together.

In the meantime, Mr. Creepy remains on display at the Seattle business, no doubt keeping a close eye on everyone and everything that comes through the door, waiting and hoping for the return of his love.

Letta Me Out!

Australian Kerry Walton grew up in Wagga Wagga, New South Wales. There was an old abandoned house on the street where he spent his childhood years. Kerry and his friends avoided the place, adhering to the popular legend that the old building was haunted, and hence, dangerous.

Walton grew up and left his hometown, starting a life of his own elsewhere in Australia. It was 1972 when he found himself returning to his hometown. Sadly, the visit was due to the death of Kerry's grandmother and the funeral services he went to attend.

There on the street he recalled so fondly sat the abandoned house. Still as dilapidated as he remembered, though in his adulthood it was not as frightening.

Curiosity, and perhaps the need to confront a childhood fear, drove Kerry to visit the old house during his time at home. Flashlight in hand, he pierced the darkness of the crumbling structure. One of his hobbies was collecting vintage bottles, and Walton thought the old place could yield a treasure trove for his collection. He made his way through the house carefully, mindful of the risky conditions, and searched the dark nooks and crannies hoping to make a discovery. He would end up with much more than he bargained for.

Having no luck finding items in the rooms of the house, Kerry decided to expand his search and venture under the home itself.

It was there, while pushing through the dust and dirt of the decrepit building, that Walton suddenly saw a face peering back at him through the cobwebs. Shocked and startled, he jerked back, almost knocking himself out as his head slammed into a floor beam above him.

At first, Kerry thought he had stumbled upon the body of a dead child. He aimed his flashlight at the figure, bracing himself for the unsettling possibility of such a grim discovery, only to find he had discovered not a decomposing human body, but a doll.

As Walton reached out and retrieved the doll, he discovered its clothing was crumbling and falling away. He wondered how the wooden doll had survived for so long stuck under the home. For that matter, he wondered how and why the doll had ended up under the old abandoned house in the first place.

Inspecting the figure, Walton was surprised to discover that the hair on the doll was made from real human hair. However, his real surprise came when he realized that the doll's scalp could be removed to reveal a "brain" inside the head of the figure.

Intrigued by his unusual find, Kerry decided to leave the house and take the antique doll with him.

After his grandmother's funeral services, Walton bid farewell to Wagga Wagga and set off for the journey home. He had driven to the town along with his brother, and the two of them would also make the return trip together. Kerry packed his bags, tossed the strange doll in an old travel bag, and threw it in the back of the van along with his other luggage. As the brothers started their return trip, Kerry relaxed in the passenger seat and tried to get some sleep while his brother drove.

Sometime later, Kerry was awoken by his brother nudging him. There were strange sounds coming from the back of the van and his brother was disturbed. The noises it seemed, were coming from the old travel bag containing the doll. Looking into the back of the van, it appeared to the brothers that the doll was moving around on its own, perhaps trying to escape the confines of the bag that held it.

Kerry tried to brush the situation off, and to put his brother

117

at ease, he took over at the wheel, completing the rest of the drive by himself. The odd sounds continued behind him the entire time, making the already long drive a nerve-wracking experience.

Once he reached his home, Kerry opened the bag to inspect the doll, unsure what he would find. Despite the weird sounds during the trip, everything seemed normal with the doll and the bag. Perhaps it had all been a case of overactive imagination.

Walton took the doll inside, ready to show his find to his family. However, when his dog saw the creepy doll, the animal became vicious, growling and barking hysterically at the figure.

It wasn't just the animals in the home that reacted to the doll. Kerry's family complained about the doll and said it seemed to always be looking at them with cold, dark eyes. Guests who stopped by the Walton home to pay a visit hated seeing the doll. Many of them would scream out when in its presence. Each person stated they found the doll extremely disturbing.

Walton's children tried playing with the doll. During the daytime, things were fine, however, at night, the doll frightened them, and they could be heard screaming and complaining about it watching them.

Fear caused the family to keep the figure at a safe distance. Kerry decided it would be best to store the doll under his house. He tucked it away and tried to forget about it.

On occasion, however, the family would awaken in the middle of the night hearing a voice screaming out from beneath the house. In a chilling tone, it cried:

"Letta me out! Letta me out!"

Walton began to call the doll "Letta." A month after his trip and the discovery of the doll, Walton learned that the old, abandoned home had been torn down. He found it odd timing since the house had stood for well over two hundred years. If he hadn't taken the time to explore it when he did, Letta would never have been found, and likely would have been destroyed during the demolition of the building. Walton now believes the doll itself may have "called" him to rescue it.

Five years passed by and the Waltons decided to sell their home. Needing money for the purchase of a new house, Kerry elected to retrieve the doll and try to sell it.

It was obvious to Kerry the doll was a very old item and he felt it might have some value as an antique or collectible. He decided to take Letta to a museum in Sydney to see if he could get any further information. He put the doll in his car and headed to the museum. What was supposed to be a day of clear, sunny skies, suddenly became a rainy downpour. Walton would come to learn that whenever Letta is taken outside, rain inevitably begins to pour.

Kerry made it to the museum and spoke with officials. On examination, experts at the Sydney museum determined the doll was between 170 and 200 years old, based mainly on the age of the nails used in the doll's shoes.

From their inspection of the figure, officials also came to believe the doll was the work of a Romanian Gypsy craftsman. The gypsies of that period were known to utilize effigies for a process they called "spirit transference," a technique wherein the souls of the recently departed would possess dolls as homes.

Armed with his new, historical knowledge about the doll, including its age and rarity, Walton listed the item for sale in hopes of getting a large amount of money from it. In short order, an offer was made, and a sale price agreed on.

Although Kerry was ready to sell the doll, Letta was not done with the Walton family. The doll's strange power was about to show itself again.

Walton set out to make the transaction and be rid of the creepy doll. As before, once he took Letta out and got into his car, the skies opened, and rain began to pour. Things got very strange when Kerry arrived at the buyer's home. He found himself paralyzed and unable to even get out of his vehicle. Frozen in place, Walton sat for what felt like hours, chills running up and down his back. He knew it was the influence of the doll and that he wouldn't be able to get out of his car. After a time, Walton resolved in his mind that he would keep the doll. He was then able to move enough to pull away from the buyer's home. As he continued driving away, Walton discovered the paralysis had left his body.

The doll quickly attracted the attention of the media and Kerry and his strange doll began making appearances on television shows. Every crew that encountered the doll felt uneasy around it and had bizarre experiences. Some experienced fear, others overwhelming sadness when in the doll's presence.

Walton and Letta made the rounds, appearing on numerous talk shows. One host of a popular, daytime program arranged a meeting between the doll and a highly regarded psychic. The doll arrived on a rainy day at the psychic's office. A painting immediately fell off the wall and a clock in the office stopped.

The psychic took the doll and held it on her lap. A film crew documented the interaction that unfolded as the doll's head slowly started to turn of its own accord. Everyone in the room saw the movement and heard the sounds of Letta's wooden neck creaking with the turn. It was far too much for one of the cameramen in attendance who turned completely white and ran out the door.

The psychic said she could feel the presence of a child, trapped inside the antique doll. She claimed the spirit was that of a six-year-old boy who had drowned during a storm in Romania. It was the boy's grieving father who had fashioned the doll himself and had his son's soul transferred into the wooden figure.

The psychic further believed the child had remained confused and frightened throughout the centuries. She believed it was an Australian immigrant who was responsible for bringing the doll to Wagga Wagga, and placing it under the old house where Kerry Walton later discovered it.

According to renown psychic June Cleeland:

"Gypsies of the 1800s believed strongly in spirit transference and making dolls through which a human soul could make worldly sanctuary after death.

Mr. Walton lives in fear of his wooden marionette, but several mediums have told him he must never try and get rid of it or he will be beset with bad luck. It's malevolent, grinning face, human hair, and glass eyes with prominent blood veins, are something you won't forget in a hurry."

During the filming of another show, one with more than two hundred viewers on a rainy day, a crowd gathered around the doll only to hear a woman screaming as Letta's head again started to turn on its own.

On yet another occasion, Walton and Letta were doing a show at a local grocery store. The shoppers were shaken when a woman, one not even in the show's audience, but from the back of the store, started screaming, *"There's an evil presence in here!"* After crying out, the woman suddenly passed out.

Letta has been known to cause terror in those who see him, but apparently, the doll's energy has a much wider range of influence.

Although many people state they believe the doll is evil or possessed, Walton himself has never reported direct, evil experiences related to Letta. In fact, after finding the doll, Walton says his luck changed for the better and his collectibles business began to boom.

Letta continues to live with the Walton family in Queensland. Dogs still don't like the doll and guests still complain about its unyielding gaze. Pictures continue to slide off the walls and whenever the doll is taken out of the home, the inevitable rain begins to pour. But the family seems content with their role as Letta's keeper. In February 2016, Kerry Walton's granddaughter, Hayleigh, posted a message about Letta on an internet thread about the doll. She states:

"This doll is haunted, I should know because I am Kerry Walton's Granddaughter and have been brought up with him as well as my siblings and extended family. We don't like to think of it as we are stuck with him, he is a family member. I have a strong attachment to Letta and have never had bad luck. My Grandparents Kerry and Evelyn Walton would never sell him or do anything to take him from his new family. We all love him, and he will always be a part of our family. I have witnessed strange things including his eyes changing color and he always wriggles on my lap when I hold him, but I am used to it and it doesn't frighten me anymore."

Sarita

The Nunez family in El Callao, Peru, is terrified. For seven years, they've been in the possession of a haunted doll. One they claim makes strange noises, moves of its own accord and leaves bruises and scratches on their children. Oddly, they refuse to part with the cursed doll.

According to Mr. & Mrs. Nunez, the doll was a gift from a relative who has since passed away. The incidents involving the doll happened soon after the relative died.

Angie Nunez, 20, feels the presence of the doll, or at least, something attached to it:

"Every night, I feel as though somebody is looking at me from the corner of the room."

The young woman says she's also heard three knocks on the door of her wardrobe, yet no human was present to make the sound.

Angie's mother, Ivonne, says the doll moves around on its own at night. She also claims that if anyone tries to move the doll, it makes what she describes as "a praying sound."

The doll's favorite target however, seems to be Steven Nunez, 18. He reports:

"Last week, I woke up with scratches on my neck and on my back."

The blonde haired, blue eyed doll, called "Sarita," also purportedly causes strange light manifestations in the home.

The Nunez family called in Soralla de los Angeles, a medium and "angel expert," in an attempt to get some answers. During her investigation, she detected the presence of a "mysterious woman" in one of the rooms of the home. According to Ivonne, the spirit is that of her sister-in-law who committed suicide in the room.

Soralla also reported an evil presence dwelling in the doll itself. An evil that intended to bring harm to the family. The medium performed a cleansing ritual to protect the house and to make the spirits leave. Purportedly, dozens of circular lights appeared as she conducted the cleansing.

The story of Sarita, dubbed the "Peruvian Annabelle," gained a lot of attention in the spring of 2017 when it was picked up by online news sources in the UK.

The tale has proven controversial however. Some stories reported conflicting information regarding the original source of the doll. Was it a gift from a nephew? A sister-in-law? And were the children really as old as 18 and 20, or were they younger?

Some people believe the entire story was concocted as a ploy to take advantage of the success of the Annabelle films. Others are convinced the tale is a true account.

Whatever the case, it wasn't the only "haunted doll" story to come out of Peru in 2017. A month after Sarita's story was zipping around the World Wide Web, another account was posted about a purportedly possessed doll in Cusco. The Cusco story too was picked up by various UK news outlets. The video that accompanied the account showed a doll responding despite having its batteries removed. This story proved even more controversial then the tale of Sarita.

Ultimately, while the stories are intriguing, without someone pursuing a direct investigation, we are left with only brief information from the news stories.

The Doll in the Window

Janesville is a small town in Waseca county in southern Minnesota. The town was incorporated in 1870, and has remained small with a current population of just over two thousand citizens. Janesville sits at the intersection of Old Highway 14 and County Road 3. It's a quiet town, normal by all standards, and yet like many other slices of small town America, it has some quirky stories and a creepy legend.

It was a quiet, average day in Janesville in 1976, when an odd, porcelain doll appeared in the attic window of a downtown home. A man named Ward Wendt lived alone in the home, and it was later learned he had placed the doll in the window himself. However, the real question that has long plagued residents of Janesville; Why did he put the doll there?

For many years, the doll peered out of the small, square attic window that faced the street. Local children grew to fear the doll, claiming its expression would change and that it watched them closely if they passed by the house. Eventually, the rumor in town was the toy was haunted, and the mystery of the Janesville Doll grew.

Over the years, the story of the doll in the window spread through the surrounding towns, throughout the region, state, and eventually, it was known far and wide. Curiosity seekers would make a point to detour through Janesville just to catch a glimpse of the creepy doll and, perhaps, spot it moving or staring at them.

The Janesville Doll became a full blown urban legend, and as with many such tales, numerous versions of how and why the doll came to be placed in the window sprung up.

One story claims a young girl living in the house ran away from home. In a state of despair, the girl's parents placed the doll in the window as a sign to their daughter that there would always be a place for her if she chose to come back.

Many versions of the tale involve the death of a young girl in the home, usually the homeowner's daughter. How exactly she perished changes depending on the version of the story.

In some tales she died from a fatal fall on the stairs, or from another tragic accident. Some say she developed a sudden illness that proved fatal and the doll was placed in the window as a memorial to the lost life.

There are other, darker twists on the story too. Some versions state the girl was abused by her family and locked away in the attic room where she would sit for hours, staring out of the window and dreaming of freedom. In this version, the girl met her end either from neglect and starvation, or in a state of despair, she hung herself from the rafters in the attic.

There are even variations on the variations. In some tales the girl is hated by the townspeople for some reason. After being bullied for a time the girl took her own life rather than face her tormentors. In this version, the doll was placed in the window to remind people to be kind to one another, lest tragedy strike.

Even darker twists on the story claim the girl was being abused by her father and that it was he who killed her, later placing the doll in the window out of remorse. Purportedly, her body is buried somewhere on the property.

If you think stories about the doll couldn't get any stranger—they do. A bizarre take on the tale delves deeply into the demonic realm.

In this history of the Janesville doll, a young girl living in the home was possessed and met her fateful end during an attempt to exorcise the demon that possessed her. At the girls' death, the demon exited her body and took up residence in her doll. It's believed that anyone who stares into the eyes of the doll for too long risks becoming possessed themselves. The demon is simply biding its time, waiting for the right opportunity—and victim.

Stories about the doll have long been popular at regional high

124

schools and at the local college campus in Mankato. The Minnesota State Mankato student newspaper wrote an article about the creepy doll, using the legend as a way to warn students about the evils of the world.

There was also a short film made about the doll that includes interviews with various townspeople and explores the legends and stories that have grown up around it.

"That creepy doll put Janesville on the map," claims one local resident. Indeed, everyone in the region knows about the doll and has something to say about it. Legend trippers and curiosity seekers have gone to the town for years, snapping photos of the doll peering out of the attic window. Schoolchildren on buses would crowd around the windows when passing the home, catching a glimpse of the doll and telling versions of the tales associated with it.

Often, those who saw the doll would claim to see it move.

"It was watching us as we watched it!"

"To this day, I swear the doll turned its head and gave us a nasty glare, all because my boyfriend made a rude comment about it, poking fun at it. That doll is evil, plain and simple."

Legends and tales aside, what is the real story behind the doll in the window? Information is scant. A search of local records has to date revealed no murders or mysterious deaths in the home.

Ward Wendt, the man who placed the doll at its post in '76 stated the home had been in the possession of his family since the town was built and nothing exciting had ever occurred within it. Locals confirm the Wendt family owned the property from the time the town was founded. Beyond the mysterious doll, no one recalls anything ever occurring on the property that would have created paranormal conditions.

Ward Wendt himself was born in the home and lived in it until his old age. He was an antique collector and was especially fond of trains with a big collection of train memorabilia.

Wendt passed away in 2012 at the age of 84, taking the secret of the Janesville Doll to his grave. Or, maybe not.

There's a final twist to this strange, Minnesota urban legend.

The year the weird doll appeared in the attic window of the Janesville home was also the United States Bicentennial. There were celebrations and special events being held around the country, including one in Janesville, where a special ceremony was held in a local park. During the celebration, a time capsule was buried in a concrete vault. Purportedly, one of the items placed in the capsule was a note written by Ward Wendt himself. It's a written statement that reveals his reason for placing the doll in his attic window.

The time capsule is scheduled to be unearthed and opened one hundred years after its placement. We may, possibly, have an answer to the mystery of the Janesville doll—in 2076!

Is there a deep mystery behind the Janesville Doll? A tragic death? An encounter with the demonic? Or, did Wendt place the doll in the window with the sole purpose of creating an urban legend?

Whatever the case, the doll in the window put Janesville on the map and created a unique legend known far and wide.

After Ward Wendt passed away in 2012, the doll ended up in the hands of the Janesville Historical Society and was placed in a display case in the town's public library. People still come to Janesville to catch a glimpse of the doll and take photos of it in hopes of catching something strange.

A Facebook page called "Doll in the Window" was launched, but it only received attention for a brief time after Wendt's death. Perhaps excitement will build when we get closer to 2076, until then the doll sits quietly in its glass case, holding on to the secret of its time in the Janesville window.

Pupa the Haunted Italian Doll

There's a strange European doll known as "Pupa." The name Pupa itself is the Italian word for doll. Created in the 1920s, the doll was made in the likeness of her owner, a child born in Trieste, Italy. Pupa is fourteen inches tall. Her head, arms and legs were all fashioned with felt. Her hair was made with hair from the child's head.

The little girl who received Pupa became strongly attached to the doll from the very start. The doll was the girl's constant companion as the child and her family traveled extensively throughout Europe and the United States. Often, the doll would be clad in clothing that matched the little girl's outfits.

Towards the end of the Second World War, the child's grandmother passed away. As a way to honor and remember her, the little girl had a button that belonged to her grandmother sewn onto a blue dress that Pupa often wore.

The little girl always kept her special doll close at hand. Family members frequently noted how lifelike the doll appeared when looking back at pictures of the girl and her companion. They may have found it odd, but none of them seemed alarmed about the matter. After all, Pupa made the girl happy and the child treated the doll as if it were alive, speaking to it often and treating it as her friend and confidante.

As the girl grew and aged, she continued to keep Pupa, and when as a young woman she moved to the United States, Pupa went with her. The woman passed away in 2005, but before she did, she passed along stories about her companion Pupa, including an incident when the doll saved her life. She told her grandchildren that Pupa was no mere doll, but a living entity with a mind of its own. She also told her descendants that Pupa spoke to her.

After the woman passed away, Pupa fell into the hands of remaining family members who decided to keep her as a family treasure. Still dressed in her blue dress, with a button from the woman's grandmother, and a big, blue bow in her hair, the doll was placed into the safety of a glass case. The family wanted to honor and remember both their mother and her grandmother by putting Pupa in a safe place where she could be seen and not damaged.

Apparently however, Pupa didn't care for being locked in a confined space and she began to make it clear she was more than just an average doll. Shortly after she was placed in the display case, a family member noticed small smudges on the glass. She decided to clean the glass and blew some hot air onto the spot to better see and wipe the smudges away. She received quite a shock when her breath revealed what was on the glass; what appeared to be the impression of a child's fingertips, and a pair of words written beside them: *"Pupa hate."*

From that time forward, Pupa remained active. If she wanted someone's attention, there would be a rapping sound from the cabinet, the doll was apparently knocking on the glass. At times, in fact, people heard the tapping sound on the glass, and when they turned to look, there was Pupa with her hands pressed against the inside of the cabinet. One report even states the doll shattered the glass cabinet once in an effort to show her anger at being locked away.

Family members and friends state that Pupa will change position when no one has touched her. At times, she will be sitting normally, then suddenly, someone notices the doll's legs are crossed. Even stranger, her facial features are known to change their expression.

It's also said Pupa has gotten out of the glass cabinet and has been found sitting outside the case. Sometimes other items are placed in the display case with the doll. If she doesn't like them, Pupa will push the items away from her.

One family member reportedly witnessed the doll rise to her feet and move around inside the glass case. The witness grabbed a camera and filmed the doll's movement. Afterwards, several family members sat down to review the footage. A strange fog obscured the footage, and within it, the words *"Pupa no"* appeared.

The same man captured Pupa's movements on video on two other occasions, but each time, when he went to review the footage, there was nothing but a milky blur that obscured the doll and everything else.

Apparently, Pupa doesn't want her movements caught for prosperity.

What turned Pupa from a beloved confidante and constant companion into a troubling, haunted doll? Did she become despondent after the loss of her friend, the woman she spent so many years with? Did she become angry at being relegated to a glass case, locked away from people and displayed as a mere object?

At this time, it's unlikely anyone will be able to delve further into the doll and its possible paranormal energies. No one knows where Pupa is now. The family has decided to keep the doll's location a secret. They say they are doing so to protect themselves, the mother's memory, and of course, the doll Pupa.

The Haunted China Doll

"I don't know why I decided to buy the dolls. It was a bit strange, but at

the time, I didn't think much about it. Even that's unusual. They were really cheap, they were only £5 I think, and I thought they would probably be worth quite a bit of money."

So states Debbie Merrick, 50, of King's Lynn, Norfolk, UK who purchased a set of three dolls from a local charity shop. She thought the dolls were a good deal, but as she states, even she was puzzled by the purchase. Something about one of the three dolls in particular bothered her:

"It's really just the one doll with the white dress I don't like. I didn't particularly even like touching that one when I bought it. The other two I don't mind as much."

Debbie took the dolls home and placed them in her home's spare bedroom. Shortly after taking the dolls home, strange things began to happen in the Merrick household, as Debbie reports:

"The smoke alarms keep going off, and one night I heard the floorboards creaking and thought it might have been my daughter Holly up, but when I checked on her she was asleep."

A week after the dolls were brought into the home, Debbie's husband Cameron woke one morning with scratches all over his legs. The marks were red and sore, and Cameron could find nothing to explain how they had appeared. The Merrick's daughter, Holly, was convinced it was the doll that had attacked her father while he slept.

Merrick recalls the incident:

"...my husband said to me, 'I've got scratches all over my legs.' It definitely hadn't happened before. They looked a bit like cat scratches and were sore.

My husband is a complete non-believer. He's still trying to come up with an explanation. The scratches do look like they've been done by something small, like little doll hand scratches.

Holly keeps telling people that the creepy doll scratched her Dad's leg."

While Debbie herself hasn't been scratched by the doll, she also wasn't spared from creepy incidents involving it. She started having nightmares about the doll. In her dreams, she would see the doll, dragging itself along the floor towards her.

In search of answers, Merrick reached out to a friend of the family who has psychic ability. The psychic investigated and identified one of the trio of dolls as the source of the strange events unfolding at the Merrick's home. Delving further in, the psychic told Debbie it was the doll in white that was causing the smoke alarms to go off because it was moving about the house, creating sudden changes in temperature, triggering heat sensors on the smoke units.

The medium also informed the Merricks that the doll had 'something in it,' and recommended the family not continue keeping the doll in the house. Coming to the realization, or rather belief, that she now owned a possessed doll, Merrick wrapped the item up, placed it in a box, and locked it away in a shed. As a further safety measure, Merrick piled other items on top of the box that contained the creepy, animated doll.

But it wasn't the end of the story, nor of the doll's activity.

Two days after storing the doll away in the shed, Debbie was back in the building, searching for another item, when she discovered the doll had moved. Inspecting the figure, she found it had also removed the small, pearl necklace that it wore. As she recalls:

"The other day I had to go into the shed to get something, and when I looked in the box the necklace on the doll was completely off and the doll was in a different position, I'm sure. When I'd packed it away I'd made sure the necklace was wrapped around its neck about four times. I was quite scared of it to be honest. I just kept thinking 'how?' I didn't want to touch it and when I had to touch it I felt sick."

Enough was enough. Determined to be rid of the doll, Debbie took a series of photographs of it, so she could list if for sale on eBay. After taking the photos, she promptly left the shed and the doll.

"I don't want to go back into that shed now. I won't touch it again, it can get picked up if it's bought, and if we need to post it, my husband can package it up. If it doesn't sell, it will go back to a charity shop."

Even creating the listing for the doll proved to be a challenge. As Merrick recalls:

"I took some pictures of it because I wanted to put it on eBay, then I left it. I even struggled to upload the pictures to eBay, it was really strange, that had never happened before."

Merrick listed the haunted doll on eBay as a "Creepy China Doll," with a starting bid of only £25. The low price she states, was because she just wanted to be rid of the troublesome item. The listing contained the following description:

"...a pretty doll in a wedding outfit but very creepy, just something about it, it's fair to say we don't want it in our house anymore. It's made by franklin mint and in good condition just needs a tidy up. I bought 3 of these dolls from a second-hand shop as I thought they were pretty but no longer want them! Buyer must collect please if possible, but I will post if needed."

To the woman's surprise, the china doll sold for £866.00 ($1122.77 in US dollars).

The high price for the item really shouldn't have been too surprising. After all, the paranormal activity and purported attack by the doll had garnered some media attention. News articles and stories on the Internet go a long way in hyping attention for haunted items. Merrick herself also made an appearance on ITV's "This Morning," a popular talk show. She stated that taking the doll to the station caused some strange incidents with lights at the studio. A national television appearance helped make the doll big news among paranormal enthusiasts, and a lot of attention was put on the item when it was placed up for auction.

Still, Merrick was very happy when the doll sold and was out of her hands:

"I was so glad when the doll went, to be honest."

Debbie Merrick says she's had experiences with paranormal incidents since she was five years old, including seeing a ghost.

"It's the women in my family who experience paranormal things. In my last house, there was definitely something there. I think my dad who died recently might be trying to get in touch.

There could be something in the doll. I believe things can attach to items—that's why I have no old furniture in my house."

The Merrick's still have the two remaining dolls from Debbie's original charity shop purchase. Although there's been no activity from them to date, Debbie's husband is waiting for the day he wakes up with strange scratches again. At that point, the other dolls will be on eBay too, hopefully following their predecessor in fetching a good price at auction.

China Doll Strikes Again

August 2017

It wasn't long after Debbie Merrick sold her haunted china doll on eBay that it was in the hands of new owners. Because of the media attention the doll had garnered, a bidding war erupted when it was initially placed up for bids. Those interested in the paranormal vied for a chance to snag the haunted doll to find out if the activity would continue once it was in new hands.

The auction was won by paranormal investigator Lee Steer who got the item for the previously stated £866. Merrick wasted no time in shipping the item off to its new home in Rotherham, South Yorkshire.

Steer, 30, lives with his parents, Paul and Amy Steer. It was only two days after the creepy doll arrived at the Steer home that activity began. Lee's father, Paul, was attacked in a manner similar to the attacks that struck Debbie Merrick's husband when she owned the doll. Paul, 54, found scratches on his arm, small marks as if from the hands of a doll. As Steer reports:

"My dad was downstairs in the morning, at this point the doll was still packed away, and he heard like a tapping noise on wood. He said it was a bit unusual. Later that day, he was watching the repeat of one of our live streams with the doll. I was doing a live stream upstairs in my room.

Then he said to my mum, "My arm's hurting." He lifted up his sleeve and he had six scratches on his arm.

My mum shouted to me, "Lee, you best get downstairs—your dad's getting affected. He's got scratches on him."

Examining the scratches on his father's arm, Lee found they were very similar to those received by Debbie Merrick's husband when the couple owned the doll. He reports that his father is "a believer" and is not happy with the cursed doll being in the household.

Like the Merrick family, Lee and his family began to have other paranormal activity unfold in their home. Odd, unexplainable noises, flickering lights and more. As Lee notes:

"We were putting stuff away that weekend before it arrived and started talking about it, and all of a sudden, a picture I have on my wall called 'The Crying Boy' started swinging on its own.

We've gone months without anything unusual happening and as soon as this doll is mentioned things start happening.

I have another picture propped up on the floor. In the dark I could hear this sound, and when I put the light on and looked, the picture frame had completely dismantled itself."

It should be noted, the painting Steer refers to above, known as "The Crying Boy," is also a famous cursed object. The Crying Boy is reputed to cause fires in the homes of those who possess a copy. It shows, at the least, that Lee Steer has some familiarity with haunted and/or cursed objects. He does in fact, have a small "Haunted Objects Museum" in the home.

Steer did a live-streamed paranormal investigation focused on the doll. He started with the opening of the shipping box containing the doll. Activity was high from the start. Lights in the room began to act strangely. Viewers watching the investigation reported the doll's eyes were moving.

Paranormal communication devices Steer was using issued a number of words and statements including the name "Samantha" and the statement "strike Lee."

Steer is casual about the reported, intense activity and reports connected to the doll. He keeps the item next to his bed and continues to monitor it for activity.

"People say I've got a death wish. I need to see something to believe it. I don't believe in ghosts as such, but I do believe in paranormal activity. I want to experience the ultimate.

I've been losing my faith recently, nothing's happened for months, but then this doll came along. This is the first time I've seen this kind of activity in 15 years."

Steer believes the doll, or rather, whatever is attached to it, has an innate hatred of married men. This could explain the attacks on both his father and Debbie Merrick's husband:

"We've done some research and found out it's from America, and that kind of doll was given to newly married couples. It's difficult to prove, but we have heard from one woman who claims she had sold the doll on, and that it had come from a house of a woman who had owned a thousand of these dolls."

Steer says he and his team are looking to test the theory on married couples to see if the doll attacks other men.

Lee Steer has been in touch with Debbie Merrick, the woman he won the doll from online. She remains happy to have gotten rid of the doll, and isn't surprised at the activity Steer and his family have experienced. As she states:

"It was a real shocker when Lee messaged me to say his dad had been scratched too.

I wasn't surprised when he opened it live and was getting flickering lights. We had that in the hotel the night before we went on 'This Morning' - right above our table while we were eating downstairs, and then in our room later as it was, weird—they were flickering like crazy, only in the bit of the room the doll was in.

I know people are mocking the whole thing, but I think the fact Lee's dad was scratched too just goes to show there is something going on with that doll."

Clearly, the saga of the haunted China Doll is still unfolding. Whether or not Lee Steer will continue to keep the cursed item, or if the activity will become too intense for he and his family remains to be seen. Who will be the next victim of the small, scratching hands of the china figure?

The Devil Baby Doll

The mystical city of New Orleans, Louisiana is one of the most haunted cities in the world. It overflows with legends, from Voodoo Queens and "Rootworkers," to pirate ghosts and vampires, the city is full of magic and spirits. But lurking in the shadows of the city's back streets and alleys is a particularly creepy legend known as the devil baby doll.

Sometimes called the "Devil Baby of Bourbon Street" legend says the little monster was adopted by Voodoo Queen Marie LaVeau and even christened by the notorious Madame LaLaurie.

The story of the devil baby begins in the 1800s when a young woman from one of the city's most powerful families married a wealthy Scotsman. Heading into the beneficial marriage, the woman left an angry lover behind and he did not take the matter lightly. The scorned man sought out Marie LaVeau, the Voodoo Queen of New Orleans and paid her to work her mojo on the new bride so he could have his revenge. LaVeau laid a terrible curse on the woman. When the woman later went into labor with the Scotsman's offspring, she died at childbirth, but not before bringing forth a misshapen baby said to be the progeny of the devil himself.

The baby was a frightening sight and was scorned by those who saw it for they feared it would bring darkness into their lives. Feeling pity for the misshapen baby, the Voodoo Queen herself took the child in and cared for it. The baby was christened by the infamous Madame LaLaurie and it lived to plague the city's French Quarter for many years. Legend says when the baby passed, it was buried alongside Marie LaVeau in her vault in Saint Louis Cemetery No 1.

Other stories claim the baby lived on in a ghostly form, a child-sized devil lurking in the darkness. Citizens of the Big Easy spoke in whispered tones about the devil baby. They feared the entity and believed it hid in the shadows of the back streets and alleys, waiting to cause misfortune to any who crossed its path.

As a means of protection, the people of New Orleans began to carve images of the devil baby out of gourds. They believed that by hanging the images outside of their homes, they could prevent the real devil baby from intruding into their houses and cursing their lives.

Soon, "Rootworkers," magical practitioners of Hoodoo, started using the little devil dolls to curse people. In these cases, magic was being used in an attempt to call the devil baby's attention to specific people, so it would curse them. The carved babies would show up on the doorstep of the unfortunate target of someone's ire. It was a frightening item for one to find in front of their home.

Fear of the devil baby grew around the city. The carved dolls were primitive but were made to more closely resemble the real devil baby than were the carved gourds previously used. The dolls would be dressed in children's clothing and made to stand on their own with a stuffed body and arms that could be moved. The face of the dolls was always the same, with leering, glassy eyes, and little devil horns that protruded from the forehead. A knotted, jute tail would complete the devilish appearance. At some point, a woman who had seen the real devil baby as a child confirmed the similarity between the dolls and the real child.

It's reported that Marie LaVeau didn't approve of the use of devil baby images and laid a curse on all the dolls. A curse many believe is still active.

In fact, the notorious devil baby is still creating waves of fear and curiosity on the streets of New Orleans. In modern times, newer versions of the dolls have begun to appear around the city. It's said they are exact replicas of the original dolls used by Hoodoo practitioners and because of this, they are believed to be possessed.

Most of the old, original devil baby dolls are long gone, or sitting in family heirloom cabinets or private curio collections. On the rare occasion one has shown up on the market, the prices are usually extremely high.

Enter New Orleans artist Ricardo Pustanio who claims to own the remnants of one of the original devil baby dolls from the 1900s. Based on the artifact in his possession, Pustanio began creating his own devil baby dolls. Customers who have purchased these highly sought-after pieces say that Pustanio's dolls are haunted.

When he made his first set of devil dolls, Pustanio said when they were gathered together, whispering and rustling sounds could be heard. Thinking he should separate the dolls to quell the energy, the artist convinced several of his friends to each take a doll for safe keeping. Almost right away, Pustanio's friends all wanted to return the dolls to him, reporting strange occurrences in their homes after taking the dolls.

One person reported the devil baby moved on its own when no one was around. Left in a closet in the man's spare bedroom, he would come home to find the closet door open and the doll laying out on the carpet.

Another couple reported that the doll they were keeping overturned items and threw beads from a bead making kit around the room. No one else was in the home when the incident occurred.

Everyone who attempted to keep one of the devil dolls suffered disturbances in their homes. In fact, there have been so many reports of the dolls moving on their own and causing turmoil in the lives of those who take them, that Pustanio now sells the dolls with a "Buyer Beware" warning.

Although the artist's devil baby dolls remain highly sought after, some people who have purchased one of the modern pieces have quickly decided to sell it, disturbed at the presence that seems to follow the little dolls and the chaos that quickly erupts in their homes.

Paranormal investigator Sylvia Cross bought one of the devil babies to add to her collection of creepy dolls. Even she was disturbed by the amount of activity the thing exhibited. She reported weird shuffling sounds and the cries of a baby coming from the doll. Her cats refuse to go near the doll and won't even enter the room where it sits.

"Some objects are just 'born' for lack of a better word, with a dark soul. I think the Devil Baby is one of those objects. If you look into its eyes you can almost discern the flicker of a trapped, unhappy soul."

A disturbed, trapped soul? A dark curse from the Voodoo Queen herself? Decide for yourself. If you're brave enough, Pustanio's dolls are available. They're all one of a kind and can even be made to order, but remember, purchase at your own risk, you may be taking home a piece of the spirit of one of New Orleans' creepiest legends.

The Temple of Barbie

A pale, yellow sign with a red arrow points the way. In three languages, it states simply, "German Girl Shrine."

The sign leads to a mysterious site on a remote part of the southwest plains on the island of Pulau Ubin, in Singapore.

Although not promoted by the country's tourism board, people flock to the site with cameras in hand and alert, curious minds. Visitors to the obscure shrine also arrive bearing gifts; flowers, fruit, beer, toys, and, most frequently, cosmetics. They also come to the shrine with desires; requests for healing and blessings, prayers for money and success, and especially, requests for luck in gambling.

The actual shrine is nothing more than a small, yellow hut. In the center of the single room, is an altar adorned with flowers, incense, and the gifts visitors bring. At the center of this humble, popular altar is a single figure. A Barbie doll.

For the origins of this strange shrine with a doll at its center, we must journey back to the turn of the 20th century, specifically, the year 1914.

Tensions around the globe were high as the powder keg that would become World War One was igniting. Spies were suspected everywhere as lines were drawn and sides were chosen. In the British colonies, soldiers were on high alert and keeping a close eye on people, especially families of German descent. In the British colony of Singapore, one German couple was signaled out as potential spies and arrested by the army. While the pair were captured, their teenage daughter managed to briefly escape. Pursued by soldiers, the girl lost her footing and plunged to her death off a cliff.

A few days after the tragic accident, the girl's body was found by plantation workers. It was laying on a large stone covered in ants. The workers, a group of Chinese men, moved the girl's remains to the top of the hill and gave her a proper burial. Being Taoists, the workers put up a Chinese style temple with some coins and an iron cross to honor the girl's spirit.

In 1974, a granite quarry company took over the hill for development. The girl's remains were then exhumed and relocated to the current shrine location. A large stone near the shrine is purportedly the stone on which the girl died, it too frequently has offerings on and around it.

The origins of the shrine have undergone years of retelling and modifications, so much so that it's hard to sort out the real story from its additions.

The shrine itself has undergone renovations several times over the years, most recently in February 2015.

The current shrine has a porcelain altar that purportedly contains a lock of the girl's hair and the crucifix she wore. The items were placed in a well-decorated urn. Some reports however, state that robbers made off with the original urn containing the girl's remains. The urn was reportedly valuable because of its exquisite design and material.

The strangest twist in the legend came with the addition of the doll. As the tale goes, a man started having dreams about a young girl. In his dreams, the girl would lead him to a specific toy store where she would point at a Barbie doll on display in the shop's front window. After having the same dream three nights in a row, the man felt compelled to travel to the town and visit the store he had been dreaming of. He found the shop, exactly as it was in his dreams, and he was shocked to find that there, on display in the front window, was the exact same Barbie doll the little girl in his dreams kept pointing to.

The man purchased the doll and took it to the Shrine of the German girl, firmly believing it was her spirit that had led him to the store and the doll so he could bring it to her at the shrine. The man believes that when he placed the Barbie in the shrine, the deceased girl's spirit transferred into the doll where it remains.

Today, the small, yellow building sits nestled in the trees. Over the door is a sign that reads: "1896 Berlin Heiligtum." The Barbie doll sits in the center of the altar, adorned with yellow cloth and beads, surrounded by stacks of perfumes, cosmetics and other offerings for the spirit of the shrine. The temple has become especially popular with those seeking good luck in games of chance. Hardcore gamblers have attributed winning streaks to the spirit of the German girl and continue to make return trips to visit, and appeal to her spirit.

Modern attempts to trace the true origins of the mysterious girl and her family have come up mostly empty handed. No records of a German family named Heiligtum have been uncovered. and public records of land ownership of the period are either scarce or completely non-existent. Some researchers who have dug into the legend of the girl think her family owned a coffee plantation on the island. The plantation was located near the current Ketam Quarry at the western end of the island. According to findings, two German families named Brandt and Muhlingan owned the property where the legend was born. The true identity of the long deceased young woman still remains a mystery.

Villagers in the region have reported sightings of the German girl's ghost. Over time, she has been turned into a local deity of sorts and is addressed as "Na Du Gu Niang," which translates to the "Datuk Maiden," or "Lady Datuk."

Despite its remote location, the site has also become popular with ghost hunters who visit to investigate and look for evidence of the girl's spirit. A range of odd experiences have been reported by those who spend time at the site. Uneasy feelings, strange sounds and disembodied voices, and strange light and shadow anomalies are among the reported phenomena.

Legend says if anyone dares to spend a night alone in the shrine, they risk becoming possessed by the spirit that dwells there. Few take the risk and the haunted Barbie of Pulau Ubin continues to sit quietly in its forest home.

The Curse of Joliet

Strange laughter and cries ring out in the night, echoing through the home. While unsettling, the most disturbing thing about the sounds are their source—a doll.

Anna has the cursed doll in her possession, and although its presence is troubling, she'll never part with the figure for there's much, much more to the story. The doll is not just a haunted or cursed toy, it's a container that holds the soul of her deceased child.

The doll is known as Joliet, and for over a century, it has been passed down through Anna's family. A bizarre heirloom held by the family's women, one after the other. They have been cursed with the doll and act as guardians of the souls the figure holds captive, which at current count, numbers four boys.

Purportedly, the curse prevents the family's women from giving birth to a male heir that survives beyond infancy. For four generations, the women in Anna's family have each given birth to two children, one daughter and one son. While the births of the baby boys are without complication, and the child initially seems completely healthy, in short order, the newborn contacts a sudden, mysterious illness and, on the third day of his young life, the child dies.

The curse began when Anna's great-grandmother received Joliet as a present from a family friend. At the time, she was pregnant with her second child, a boy, and the doll was a gift to celebrate the pending birth.

What was unknown at the time was that the woman bore some hidden resentment or jealousy towards the pregnant woman. Some say the woman was unable to bear children herself and resented the fact that Anna's relative was on the way to delivering her second child. Other indications said the woman was in love with the child's father. Perhaps both were true. Either way, the woman is said to have cursed the doll to bring ill fortune and tragedy to the family.

Anna's great-grandmother gave birth to a healthy baby boy, but in three days, the child passed away. Shock and grief filled the family.

It was August of 1945 when the strange power of the cursed doll became clear. The grieving mother started to awaken, the sounds of her departed son's cries and screams ringing out in the night. Investigating the source of the unnerving sounds, the woman found that the noises were coming from the doll she had been given.

Joliet, it seemed, held the spirit of her deceased child.

The doll became a constant reminder of the family's tragic loss. The nightly cries brought back tears and memories of the lost baby. Oddly, in the midst of the disturbing realization, there was a strange sort of comfort. Knowing the boy's spirit was in the doll offered a continued connection to the child, and as long as he was in Joliet, she could care for him and have him near—at least in some form.

Anna's family believes the curse of the doll was effective and that each generation has suffered because of it. For years, the woman kept, and cared for, the haunted doll. What she did not know at the time, or indeed, for many years, was that the curse of the doll would be passed down to her daughter and to following generations.

The curse of Joliet would strike again and again, in each generation, tragedy would fall upon the infant boys born to the family's women. Each of these mothers came to realize that the spirits of their lost boys were somehow attached, or held within, the doll.

The story is always the same. The loss of the newborn boy in a matter of days after birth. The unsettling cries ringing out in the night, and the distinct understanding that the spirit is within the doll. There's another twist in the tale; only the mothers can hear the cries of their departed children. Each mother has cared for the doll just as they would for their sons, had the children lived.

The women say the cries are distinct and that they know, based on the sounds, which baby is crying out. Sometimes, there are multiple cries, and at times, the voices of all four lost children can be heard emitting from the doll at once.

Anna is the present owner of the haunted doll and the most recent member of the line to have direct experience with the curse of Joliet. She knows the names of all four souls trapped within the doll. Growing up, she knew the spirit of her dead brother was in the doll. When she became an adult and married, she too experienced a loss. Just like her predecessors, she had two children, a girl and a boy, but the boy tragically died in infancy at the three-day mark. She believes her son's spirit now dwells within the doll Joliet.

Anna says the hardest part of the curse is the knowledge that it will be passed down to her daughter and there is nothing she can do. It's a heavy burden to bear, but Anna won't risk getting rid of, or losing the doll. After all, it's the vessel for the spirits of numerous family members and she's responsible for caring for them. For now, the disturbing cycle of the cursed doll continues.

The German Doll

Boston, Massachusetts, August 1964. Single mother Irene Tucker sat chatting with two friends at the kitchen table in her two-bedroom apartment. It was ten thirty in the evening when the women heard voices coming from the bedroom of Irene's eleven-year-old daughter, Holly Anne. The disturbing thing was, they knew the little girl was alone in her room.

A rush of fear swept through Irene as she rushed to her child's room and burst through the door. There was her daughter fast asleep in bed, nestled in with two of her favorite dolls. To Irene's relief, there was no one else in the girl's room. Perhaps she had imagined the whole thing.

Going back to the kitchen, Irene's neighbor, Natalie, asked if the radio had been on in the child's room.

"No. Perhaps Holly Anne was talking in her sleep," Irene replied, trying to brush the whole matter off. The women resumed their conversation, but in short order, voices were once again heard coming from the little girl's bedroom. This time, all three women went into the hallway and quietly moved to the child's door. They stood for a moment and listened to a high-pitched female voice, one that was definitely not Holly Anne's. They listened as the voice spoke to the girl:

"Will you get up, Holly Anne—get up and talk to me!"

Irene and her friends burst through the door and turned on the lights, positive they would catch the culprit. Once again, inside the room, they only found Holly Anne, fast asleep in her bed.

The noise woke the sleeping girl who looked confused as to why her mother and neighbors were in her room. Irene tried to console the girl:

"Hush darling, go back to sleep. We thought we heard voices and we

came to see if you were okay."

Holly Anne quickly replied:

"Of course I'm okay, Mommy. You probably heard Betsy calling me. She always tries to wake me up and get me to play with her."

One of the women asked who Betsy was, at which point, Holly Anne held up one of her dolls.

"This is Betsy. Say hello to Mommy's friends, Betsy."

The puzzled women left the room and stood for a moment in the hallway. None of them seemed to know what to say. Before they could speak, voices were once again heard from Holly Anne's room:

"It's about time you got up, sleepy head. Why didn't you tell those cats off—haven't they anything better to do than snoop on us?"

The women listened as the girl replied:

"I suppose not. I guess they heard us and Mommy was scared and all. You know how Mommy is."

Irene looked at her friends and told them that this time, they would surely catch whoever was in the child's room. She threw open the door and rushed in. Again, the women found only the little girl and her dolls.

They searched the entire room top to bottom, under the bed, in the closet, even outside the locked window. There was nothing, no sign of any intruder.

Irene argued with her daughter, trying to determine how the girl was tricking them all. Still, the girl claimed innocence and stated it was her doll doing the talking.

The women returned to the kitchen, exasperated and confused. They talked late into the night, discussing all the various possibilities to explain what they had experienced, and yet there was no good explanation. Irene and her friend were at a loss.

"I think this whole thing is driving me crazy. Dolls can't talk—or can they?"

Over the next two weeks, the strange incident repeated itself on three more occasions. One of the women borrowed a voice activated tape recorder and Irene hid it in her daughter's room hoping to catch more evidence. When the women listened to the tape the following day, they became convinced; somehow the doll was speaking.

Frustrated, Irene decided to end the matter. She went into Holly Anne's room late one evening and took the doll. She examined it closely, again, hoping to find an explanation, but found nothing. She carried it to her own bedroom and placed it on her dressing table.

Late that night, Irene was awoken to a scream and a loud thump in her bedroom. Startled, she jumped out of bed and turned on the light. She found the doll, Betsy, laying on the floor with its head broken.

Never again were voices heard coming from Holly Anne's room. Several weeks later, the women played the tape recording to a linguist who had heard about the strange incident. He identified the voice as one with a German accent. When Irene further examined the broken doll, she discovered markings confirming that it had been made in Germany.

The Deadly Puppet

"...without warning my throat suddenly went really tight. I've never had anyone's hands around my throat before, so it was really scary. While I was choking, I tried to wake my wife, but it took her ages to come round. When she did, I remember looking straight at the puppet sitting on the drawers near our bed and realizing it was him."

The disturbing account above is from John, a man in the United Kingdom who was the original owner of a deadly puppet he inherited from his father.

The puppet is in the likeness of an old man and was made in the 1960s. Its face is intricately carved, and it wears metallic glasses. As a traditional marionette, the puppet has cross bars and strings attached to manipulate its movements. John inherited the puppet after his father's death, but he was never comfortable with the toy. He kept the item to honor his father's memory since it was one of the man's favorite belongings.

"My first memory of it was when I was 19, it used to hang in my Dad's spare room. I never liked it and people would never sleep in the same room as

the puppet because there was a weird atmosphere in the room."

Shortly after he inherited the toy, John and his wife began to experience paranormal activity around their home. At first the activity was minor, but it soon escalated:

"Two weeks after inheriting the puppet I started to have really bad headaches and feeling dizzy, which I never thought could be the puppet. I struggled to sleep because I'd have nightmares where an old man would hold me down or would be sitting at the edge of my bed.

I cleared out all of my dad's belongings apart from the puppet, which I left on the drawer by my bed for some reason and that night it felt like I was being choked. I was wide awake in bed and thought I saw a shadow move from one side of the window to the other and worried something was trying to scare us."

Concerned for he and his wife's safety, John contacted Jayne Harris, a paranormal investigator in the West Midlands who specializes in haunted objects.

Harris investigated John's house in an effort to find the cause of the couple's supernatural troubles. When the man presented the puppet to Harris, she ran an EMF (Electro-Magnetic Field) meter over the item. The device picked up wild readings from the puppet. As John watched, *"...the meter started flashing and beeping."*

The readings confirmed the puppet was an item of concern and John promptly asked Harris to take the doll away, despite the fact it was something from his father.

After the investigator left with the puppet, John and his wife felt much better and more comfortable in their home.

In an interview on the Website Vice UK, Harris talked about her personal experiences right after obtaining the haunted puppet:

"The day I got it back home I put it in the cabinet in my basement and closed the door. Five minutes later, when I was upstairs, I heard a bang. A tin of paint had fallen and smashed the cabinet, and there was paint all over the floor. The doll was just sitting there. It looked really creepy."

Jayne also reports that once she took the puppet home, she began having headaches and difficulty sleeping, both conditions that plagued the doll's former owner, John.

"Days later, my three-year-old daughter started saying, 'Shhh, mummy, John is asleep.' When I asked who John was she told me he was her friend. I thought, 'Okay, children have imaginary friends, it's not unusual.' Then, a few days later, she came running into the kitchen crying and said, 'Mummy! Mummy! John shouted at me...' This made me feel really uncomfortable..."

Harris decided to conduct some controlled experiments on the puppet and placed it in a sealed, glass container blessed with holy water:

"We've always kept the puppet in a sealed blessed cabinet as it's a safe zone. It also means we can keep our experiments as controlled as possible."

As a further control, the cabinet was set up in a basement, an area with no human activity. Harris and her team aimed night vision cameras at the case and proceeded to film the toy each night for three months. Under these conditions, the team caught what they believe is amazing footage of paranormal activity: the puppet moving on its own.

It was in the dead of night when cameras caught the wooden toy's operating cross slowly moving upright and then crashing down into one of the glass sides of the sealed case. After rising slowly, it stops at a 90-degree angle to the bottom of the sealed glass case, before falling over. Harris says the footage left her dumbstruck:

"I've never had anything as exciting as this. I've caught pictures of mists, orbs, and shadows, but nothing as physical as this video evidence. Normally, you expect to see an orb or shadow, but as soon as I saw a bit of movement and a glint from the metal hooks it made me jump and I knew we'd recorded something important."

Harris reports the footage was taken using a standard, and fairly old, Sony camcorder set to night vision mode. In an interview with UK based blog, "Hayley is a Ghost," Harris provides further details on the conditions of the video:

"I frequently set up trigger object experiments too with the use of motion detection. Even I wasn't present at the time of the recording. We set up at 11.30pm and the tape runs using long play until roughly 3am. The Daily Mail unfortunately cropped the footage to exclude the time log and date. It was taken at 2.05am. As you can imagine reviewing up to 3 hours of night vision footage is quite a task. Usually I'm listening out for sounds, or watching for shadows/something around the object. What I did not expect was to see the object itself moving. Although I have always believed in some

way that spirits not only exist but can manipulate physical objects."

Harris says that prior to the footage, there were some anomalous sounds such as bumps and knocking around the puppet, but nothing definitive until the video.

"The cabinet has no doors, so you would have to physically lift all four sides and the base off to move it, there are not any holes or space for anything to sneak in there either. Now we're going to keep filming with motion sensors as this is just one video and we want to build a bigger picture."

Harris and her team often utilize psychic mediums in their research to gain more information they can then verify with further documentation. With all the activity around the puppet, she reached out to have someone psychically read the doll. The medium reported that the puppet has the spirit of an old man attached to it. The psychic further claimed the spirit in the marionette was "mocking the team" by demonstrating that it could move the puppet when and how it pleased, despite being physically locked in a case covered with spiritual protections.

Harris is not especially phased by the concept that a spirit may be moving in and out of a physical cabinet:

"Our ultimate goal is to find out as much as we can about the spirit and then try to understand why he is still here. The container is only a physical thing so in theory something that's not of the physical world can pass in and out."

When Harris informed the puppet's former owner, John, about the footage, he wasn't surprised:

"The fact that there's video evidence now makes me uncomfortable to be honest, I wouldn't watch it as I don't need any more proof that it was haunted. I lived with the puppet for months and it did more than enough to convince me."

Of course, doubters came out in droves when Harris posted the footage, claiming the video was a hoax, or simple movement caused by an outside force. After many years investigating haunted objects, Harris, a trained psychologist, is used to the skeptics and doesn't stress about them:

"For us, there is no point in faking your own evidence as it's only tricking yourself—this footage is real. Of course, I'm aware that no evidence will ever be enough to convince some people, however, in sharing my footage

I'm not trying to convince anyone. Believers believe, skeptics don't. I know how long I had the goosebumps on the morning of 13th July when I reviewed the footage!

Believe me, I don't share my evidence lightly. I have to be sure. I know I leave myself open to criticism but who doesn't. My view is that those with an interest in and some knowledge of the paranormal will feel it worth seeing."

Good advice for any paranormal investigator to follow. In the meantime, the deadly puppet watches and waits for its next opportunity to demonstrate its power.

The Troubled Doll

In his book, "Possessed Possessions," author Ed Okonowicz recounts a tale he calls "The Troubled Doll." The story was told to him by a retired military man in Aberdeen, Maryland.

Chuck Palmer, and his wife Kathy, were fond of shopping at yard sales, flea markets and antique stores, looking for unique and vintage items. Their small house held many such objects gathered over the years, but nothing ever caused them turmoil of a paranormal nature until they brought home a doll wearing a silk dress.

The couple snagged the doll for a bargain price while browsing a shop in Havre de Grace, Maryland. Chuck recalls that he expected the price on the doll to be at least a hundred dollars and was surprised when the clerk quoted them much lower:

"When she said $10, Chuck recalled, 'I said to myself, My God! There's more than that much in the silk of the dress. Kathy bought it right away. She couldn't believe the price.'"

There was one very curious thing about the doll. Something not found on a normal toy: Its feet were nailed into wood. As Chuck recalls:

"...its feet had been nailed into a small block of wood, which had been wrapped in the same white material as the dress. Underneath the mass of material, it wore only one yellow shoe, the other lost long ago. Through the top of each foot was a hole that protruded into the sole, a permanent reminder of where the nails had been driven that secured the feet to the block of wood."

Nevertheless, the couple took the doll home and Kathy placed it on top of the television set, making it the center piece of the room. In short order, odd things began to occur in the house. The Palmer children reported they felt the doll's eyes following them around the room. Chuck dismissed the notion, noting the glassy appearance of the doll's eyes and assuming it was a trick of the light. But there were other incidents too, the children started hearing what they described as the sound of "roller skates" in the hallway and saw doorknobs moving on their own accord.

Kathy relocated the doll to the bedroom, placing it on the bed, but when it wouldn't set up properly, she asked Chuck to remove the block of wood from the doll's feet:

"I tell you, thinking back on it now," he said, "I didn't feel right about taking that block of wood off. But, the doll seemed to fit in there real nice, sat real comfortable on the bed."

It was after this incident things began to pick up in the Palmer household. Something, it seemed, had been unleashed by the removal of the block of wood. The peak of the activity was a manifestation witnessed by Chuck. He had turned in for the night and was by himself in the bedroom. He moved the doll from its spot on the bed to the corner of the room where it usually sat. Once his head hit the pillow, he heard sounds and turned around:

"I turned to see a little girl...about 5 years old. She had blond hair, parted completely in the middle, and cut high in the front and back. She was settin' in the corner, only 10 feet away, and there was light, more like a glow, but she looked fleshly. Like she was real. She was there for a few seconds. Just settin' there rockin' with the doll."

No one else witnessed the apparition, but it was part of a series of continued, creepy incidents in the home. The Palmers became very concerned about the ghostly activity and sold many antique items they had on hand in the event something else was causing the trouble. What they didn't sell was the doll. When Okonowicz asked Chuck why they had kept the item, the man answered that he didn't know.

Talk of getting rid of the doll seemed to produce other manifestations and it wasn't long before things escalated. Kathy was struck by a swing that flew five feet off its base and hit her in the side, leaving a bad bruise.

For a time, Chuck locked the doll in a trunk and activity quelled.

He later carried the doll to his son's house and for a time it was there. When Okonowicz interviewed the man, and saw the doll, it was being kept in a tool shed at the back of the family's property. Chuck told Ed the home stayed free of activity if the doll was not inside. Reflecting on the weird experiences he'd had, Chuck told the man:

"Sometimes I think it was telling me, 'No! I don't want to go.' If I knew what to do for it, within reason, to give it peace, I would do it. But it doesn't talk. It doesn't write notes."

The Voodoo Zombie Doll

Those interested in spirits, the paranormal, and oddities in general keep the bustling trade in haunted objects moving online. Often they buy the objects with little to no background information or documented history of the activity that surrounds the item. Most listings state clearly that activity is not guaranteed, in other words, buyer beware! You may or may not be buying a genuinely haunted object.

In 2004, a woman in Galveston, Texas purchased a purportedly haunted doll on eBay. It has come to be known as the "Voodoo Zombie Doll." According to the listing for the doll, it was originally made in New Orleans, hence the potential Voodoo connection. The details listed on the seller's site claimed the doll was "very active" and "almost alive."

The doll was shipped in a metal box, along with a list of rules that were to be followed by anyone possessing the doll. First on the list was the specification that the doll should never be removed from its silver container.

The new owner ignored the list of rules and promptly removed the doll from its case. In short order, she regretted her decision. She reported that the doll began to haunt her dreams, plaguing her each night while she slept. She further claimed the doll began to attack her repeatedly.

Wanting to rid herself of the cursed item, the woman re-listed it on eBay. The doll sold, and she shipped it off to a new owner. However, the buyer reported that only an empty box arrived. The doll reappeared in the woman's house as if she had never boxed it up. Frustrated, the woman again listed the doll on eBay, only to have the entire episode play out again in the same manner, an empty box, a teleporting doll back in her home. She tried many times to rid herself of the doll, only to have the same scenario replay.

After owning the haunted doll for several years, the woman was finally able to pass it off to a ghost hunter who currently owns it and is conducting research on the item.

The doll is a mass of string and cloth, not an attractive item at all and certainly nothing a child would be inclined to play with. Little is known about the origin of the doll beyond the account that it was made in New Orleans. Is it possessed? Cursed? Was it utilized for black magic?

The mystery may never be solved. As to the woman who had so much trouble getting rid of the doll, she claims she is still plagued with spirit activity since owning the item.

The Devil's Bride, Photo by author.

Final Thoughts

Modern interest in all things paranormal has led to a different eye being cast on the age-old doll.

On a regular basis, "new" haunted dolls surface. Some are dusty antiques pulled from forgotten chests and boxes, others are of more recent manufacture, and some are anomalies, strange handmade figures or ritual items that perhaps weren't intended to see the light of day.

Investigators probe and prod them, and many end up in museums or personal collections of haunted objects.

With the wide range of how and why supernatural evidence can manifest from dolls, it should be no surprise to realize there's not one "answer" to define the nature of a haunted doll.

Over my many years investigating the paranormal, I've had many encounters with strange dolls. I've never had a personal fear of them, rather, a curiosity and interest in their unique properties and their potential as storehouses of otherworldly energy.

I personally believe dolls can indeed be repositories for yet undefined energies, and hence, "haunted." I also believe some reportedly haunted figures are simply empty vessels that by happenstance or appearance fall into the "creepy" category.

While some of my experiences around dolls in haunted locations have been quite strange, a recent series of events involving a haunted doll that came into my possession bears noting.

In 2017, I received a doll from the northeast. Dressed in a bridal gown, the doll is a vintage 1950s item that was found by a man hired to do residential clean outs.

The doll was found in the attic of a home in Ohio and the man who collected it found the item disturbing. The eyes, he said, were always watching him. Rather than bring it into his home, the man put the doll in his barn until he could pass it on to a dealer in oddities.

The doll's creepy factor was raised when I discovered it had been found sitting on the point of a pentagram. Someone, it seemed, had been using the figure for ritual magic work. Other items were found within the pentagram that I won't discuss here.

The woman I received the doll from told me she had it sitting by a painting in her shop. Apparently, the doll didn't like the painting, (which was of another doll), and the woman would constantly find the picture dangling crooked on its hanger.

From the start, there were odd things around the doll. It was shipped at the same time, and from the same location as another, much heavier item. A few days later, I received an alert from USPS that one of the packages had been "unexpectedly delayed in transit." I assumed it was the heavy metal item, but it arrived safely and on time. Two days later, the doll showed up at my box.

En route home from the post office something more troubling occurred. Driving on the Interstate, I noticed a car in my rearview mirror, zipping through traffic at around ten miles faster than most other vehicles on the road. In short order, it was along side me on the driver's side. It suddenly slowed to pace me, and as I glanced over, the driver raised a pistol and pointed it at me. I quickly hit the brakes enough to let the vehicle outpace me, then I changed lanes and exited at the next opportunity.

It was a nerve wracking experience, to say the least, and not something that had ever happened to me before. I pulled over and took some deep breaths, then called my friend and fellow investigator Dave Spinks to tell him what had happened. Dave's a former law enforcement officer and always a good sounding board. Even he was shocked at the incident. We discussed some of the logical possibilities, but nothing made sense. I wasn't traveling in an area of high crime, and there had been no related incidents reported in the city.

Sitting in my vehicle talking to Dave, I couldn't help but have the unnerving feeling that the incident could be related to the haunted doll sitting in the box behind me. I resolved to take it to my storage unit rather than my office, until I could determine more about what, if anything, was attached to the item.

I opened the still-sealed box in the storage unit and took some photos of the doll. Spontaneously, I decided to do an EVP session with my cell phone to see if I could pick up anything. It was after hours at the storage facility, and a quick check revealed no one else in the building.

Some odd things came across on the recording. A deep voice that said, "I'm God," was by far the creepiest, but there were also anomalous knocking sounds and other voices. Over the course of three quick sessions, the knocking came across on two of the recordings, and a mix of voices talking about "the devil," "Satan," and "hurt" were heard.

Without telling Dave about the information, I sent him photos of the doll and asked him to do a remote ghost box session to see what he captured. Dave set up in an isolated area with a shack hack sitting in front of a photo of the bride. He asked questions about the doll and its new owner, and all of the responses were very dark. "Satan," "devil" and "evil" all rolled out of the box over and over. A stated intent to "hurt the owner" was repeated several times. Even without the actual doll being present, Dave was disturbed by the responses and felt they related directly to the haunted item.

Wanting to gather other, independent takes on the doll, I had two other investigators use their own methods to see what they could pick up about the item. Providing them with nothing but a photograph, the messages were consistent with the EVPs and ghost box sessions.

One woman stated firmly, "That doll was used in a magical wedding ceremony and its energy is extremely dark."

At this time, the doll remains safely locked away pending further investigation. Is it a vessel of dark energy, or something innocent that fell into a weird crossing point of unusual coincidences? Time, perhaps, will reveal more.

As in all things supernatural, there are those who believe and those who doubt. At the very least, we can be assured that for some people, dolls have a deep, psychological effect that can be disturbing and downright frightening.

For those open to the vast world of supernatural possibilities, it becomes clear that dolls are a prime vessel to be used by spiritual forces that may range from the benign to the outright evil.

I'll leave it to you to decide where you stand. But the next time you're alone in a room with a seemingly quiet doll, bear in mind there may be something more going on behind those dark, glassy eyes.

Little Horrors

Creepy Dolls in Entertainment

No exploration of haunted dolls would be complete without a look at how entertainment has made use of dolls, and the fear of dolls, as the centerpieces of horror stories.

Modern audiences are now well familiar with Annabelle and the infamous "Chucky" from the "Childs Play" franchise, but dolls have long been a staple of horrific tales. In fact, dolls were being perceived as creepy long before Hollywood put its hooks in and created movie blockbusters. In the 18th and 19th century, when dolls became more human in appearance, writers began to explore the strange boundary between toys and objects that are a bit too human.

The first notable example is "The Sandman," a story by German writer E.T.A. Hoffman published in 1816. Hoffman's story is credited as the beginning of the creepy doll genre.

The Sandman involves a traumatized young man who learns that the object of his affection is not human, but a wind-up doll. The doll is the creation of an evil alchemist who may have murdered the young man's father. Much of the story's horror centers on the deceptive human qualities of the girl/doll. The other focus of the tale is the evil of the alchemist, the doll's creator. This would prove to be a frequent theme in doll stories in the coming years.

Hoffman's story set the precedent for other 19th century horror tales involving dolls. Sigmund Freud even used Hoffman's story as a case study in his work "The Uncanny." Freud refers to Hoffman as the "unrivaled master of the uncanny in literature."

The theme of an evil master behind a doll was also present in the 1936 film, The Devil-Doll. Directed by Tod Browning of Dracula fame, the film starred Lionel Barrymore as a man wrongly convicted

Movie version of Annabelle (reproduction). Photo by author.

of murder. The "dolls" in the film are actually humans reduced to one-sixth of their size by a mad scientist. Barrymore's character, Paul Layond, uses the shrinking technique to get revenge on the people who framed him.

As entertainment, and special effects moved forward, dolls continued to be used as an effective focus of horror and creepiness. Much like the use of children in horror stories, dolls represent innocence and childhood. As a reminder of simpler times and purity, dolls are seen as something that should be comforting. When these elements become twisted and represent threats, there's an even greater psychological horror that comes into play.

By the 20th century, dolls in movies had moved from being creepy plot devices, to actual homicidal maniacs. Often, the stories entail possession of the doll by a demonic entity or the soul of a human killer.

Modern doll makers blame Hollywood for the current doll stigma, citing film headliners like Annabelle and Chucky who have terrified audiences and created a general impression that dolls are evil. They would do well to do their homework, however. As we shall see below, creepy doll movies started long before Annabelle came out of the shadows and onto the silver screen.

Granted, the success of the Child's Play films created a tidal wave of rip-offs and riffs on the killer doll, and the 1980's and 1990's saw a glut of B-movie variations on the theme. From demonic toys to killer ventriloquist dolls, the big screens and direct to video market had, and continue to have, a regular flow of creepy doll movies, creating its own sub-genre within the spectrum of horror entertainment.

It would be quite an undertaking to list all of the doll-themed movies that have come out over the years, and that is not my intent here. The list below serves as an overview of some of the highlights of this genre of films, starting with early examples.

I have focused on films that have a doll as the primary focus of the storyline and plot. This, by default, leaves out some examples that may spring to many minds, such as the creepy clown doll from 1982's hit Poltergeist, and the use of a doll in the Saw franchise.

Fair warning, the synopses below do include some spoilers, so if you haven't seen something on the list and don't want plot points ruined, it may be best to skip over the entry for now.

Entries are listed in chronological order and at last check, most of the films are available in DVD format for home viewing.

The Great Gabbo (1929)

Directed by James Cruze, a successful filmmaker from Hollywood's silent era, the Great Gabbo is, at the least, an unusual film and marks perhaps the earliest use of a creepy doll on the big screen.

The film is based on a story by Ben Hecht titled "The Rival Dummy." While not considered a horror movie per se, the film does have creepy elements and of course, it's focused around a doll, in this case, a vent dummy.

The dummy, "Otto," is controlled by the ventriloquist Gabbo. In short order, we learn that it's the ventriloquist who is the true monster of the story. Gabbo is a brilliant performer, able to make his dummy talk even while Gabbo himself smokes, drinks and even eats. But Gabbo is an abusive, ugly person and as the film unfolds, he sinks into insanity. It a classic tale of an artist driven insane by his own work.

Oddly, the film contains a number of musical breaks. It was, after all, the roaring 20's, so perhaps the studio felt the need to make full use of the new era of sound in films. The movie is certainly worth a look for those interested in the evolution of horror movie dolls, and it lays the groundwork for 1978's Magic starring Anthony Hopkins as another twisted, mad ventriloquist.

Dead of Night (1945)

Dead of Night is a British anthology film viewed by many as a classic gem of horror. The film's segment, "The Ventriloquist's Dummy" again addresses the disturbing concept of a performer losing control and going insane while believing his dummy is out to get him.

Maxwell Frere is a failing ventriloquist whose doll decides he's not a good enough performer. The dummy, Hugo, is another sinister figure that, at the time, scared the daylights out of people who viewed the movie. Numerous filmmakers, including the iconic Martin

Scorsese list the segment as an influence. Scorsese has stated that the film's vent doll is one of the scariest things he's ever seen on film.

Directed by Alberto Cavalcanti from a story by John Baines, the film was unusual for the time because production of horror movies had been banned in Britain during the war.

Dead of Night is a groundbreaking film and the ventriloquist segment has important elements that became the standard for evil doll movies that came in its wake.

The Curse of the Doll People (1961)

This Mexican horror film, originally titled "Muñecos Infernales" is also known as "Devil Doll Men." Directed by Benito Alazraki from a story by Alfredo Salazar, the film never received a lot of attention in the states, but is sought out by many horror collectors for its creepy visuals.

The story involves four men who steal a sacred idol from a temple in Haiti. The temple's priest curses the men who find themselves surrounded by evil "doll people" who begin killing their family members.

Many reviews find the film uninteresting since the story is predictable and not especially surprising. Glen Kay, writing in "Zombie Movies: The Ultimate Guide," said the film was:

"A strictly by-the-numbers exercise that must have elicited more giggles than gasps on its release."

However, the film is notable for its use of little people playing the roles of the dolls. Adorned in distorted, weird masks, the actors, as the dolls, dominate the screen each time they appear.

Paralyzed by the voodoo curse, victims in the film can only lie still as the creepy dolls crawl around in the darkness and onto their beds, killing them with small knives.

Horror aficionados who enjoy the sub-genre of creepy doll movies say the film is underrated. According to William P. Simmons, of the Website Sex Gore Mutants:

"...similar to the U.S. horror movies of the 1940's, exhibiting a lush

atmosphere and storyline…A portrait of the battle between science and superstition, Doll People is also a slice of film noir, with its beautifully photographed alleyways, shadows, and distorted angles suggesting the danger and alienation of the human heart."

✓ The Twilight Zone—Living Doll (1963)

"My name is Talky Tina and you'd better be nice to me!"

Mention creepy dolls to today's older generation, and the first one that springs to many minds is Talky Tina, the weird talking doll from an episode of classic television.

Inspired by one of the 20th century's most popular and influential dolls, "Chatty Cathy," the classic show Twilight Zone brought a frightening, talking killer doll to the small screens in 1963. Coming in the fifth season of the series, "The Living Doll" centered around an infertile step-father, played by Telly Savalas, and his resentment towards his young step-daughter.

Alone with the doll, the step-father finds Talky Tina uttering disturbing statements and threats. As the story unfolds, he attempts to destroy the doll, using various tools and implements including a blow torch, vise and circular saw. Each step of the way, the doll taunts him and finally puts an end to the man.

Rod Serling closes the episode with one of his classic narrations:

"Of course, we all know dolls can't really talk, and they certainly can't commit murder. But to a child caught in the middle of turmoil and conflict, a doll can become many things: friend, defender, guardian. Especially a doll like Talking Tina, who did talk, and did commit murder in the misty region… of the Twilight Zone."

Devil Doll (1964)

Not to be confused with the 1936 film by Tod Browning, this British outing tells the tale of "The Great Vorelli" and his dummy Hugo.

Vorelli is a former medical doctor who dabbled in mysterious

Eastern magic and was stripped of his medical license. He utilizes hypnotism in his act and as the story plays out, viewers learn that Vorelli's former assistant, Hugo was killed on stage by the performer and the man's soul transferred into the ventriloquist dummy.

A struggle for control unwinds as the evil Vorelli plots to create another doll, this one female. In a twisted ending, Hugh and Vorelli's souls switch, with the ventriloquist becoming trapped in the dummy.

The ventriloquist doll in this film is played by a living person wearing a weird costume.

Trilogy of Terror (1975)

The cult classic Trilogy of Terror presented a new twist on creepy dolls with its story about a killer Zuni fetish doll.

Karen Black stars as Amelia in a story penned by Richard Matheson. Originally written as a one woman play, the story was adapted by Matheson for the anthology film.

Amelia arrives home at her high-rise apartment after shopping. Inside one of her packages is a Zuni fetish doll. Its appearance is that of a misshapen aboriginal warrior with razor-sharp teeth and armed with a spear. A scroll that comes with the fetish contains information stating that the doll contains the spirit of a Zuni hunter named "He Who Kills." A warning on the scroll states that the gold chain adorning the figure keeps the spirit trapped inside the doll and it should not be removed. The binding chain of course, quickly falls off the figure, unleashing the vicious spirit of the killer.

Amelia finds herself in a battle with the possessed doll which ends up grabbing a kitchen knife and pursuing her around her apartment. The doll is a creepy figure and emits a crazy scream as it chases the woman about.

Black, a veteran actor, effectively pulls off the tense dynamic of a lone woman at war with something human-like, yet not human.

Magic (1978)

This now classic film set the bar high for creepy doll movies. The movie featured an all-star cast including Anthony Hopkins, Ann Margret and Burgess Meredith. It was directed by Richard Attenborough and based on a novel by William Goldman.

Charles "Corky" Withers is a failed magician whose mentor tells him he better "find a new show business gimmick." Corky vanishes then returns a year later with a magician/ventriloquist act that includes a foul-mouthed vent doll named "Fats." The act proves successful and Corky is offered his own television show. He turns it down and runs to the Catskills where a strange drama begins to unfold between the magician and his doll.

With its strong cast and solid story, Magic played well as a psychological thriller with the added element of Fats, the creepy ventriloquist doll. The conversations between Corky and his dummy Fats are unsettling, and hints of Hopkins later role of Hannibal Lecter are noticeable.

Adding to the creepiness of the story, viewers can never be completely sure of who's in control—Corky or the dummy.

There's a rumor that trailers for Magic were deemed too scary after complaints from parents, and TV spots for the film were pulled. This may be an urban legend attached to the film since there's no official record of the ads having been pulled, but it certainly adds to the mystique of this cult favorite.

Making Contact (1985)

Classified as a "horror-fantasy" film, this 1985 release from West Germany was originally titled "Joey" after the movie's central character.

The movie throws in a whole range of plot elements. The main character, a young boy named Joey, has lost his father and is attempting to contact him in the spirit world. The boy is terrorized by an evil ventriloquist dummy named Fletcher. Fletcher, it seems, is possessed by a demon. The doll also has the power to summon other demons and evil forces to threaten the boy and his friends and family.

As if that wasn't enough craziness, the boy develops the power of telekinesis!

There are other random elements in the mix too. Joey's toys come alive, including Charlie, a robot. The boy discovers Fletcher the dummy in the burned-out house of a long dead magician. The only way to end the chaos and stop the evil, demonic doll, is for Joey to journey into the spirit world and battle the forces of evil by himself.

Although it may seem one of the strange entries on this list, it's an unusual film due to its story elements, and it's an example of a foreign filmmaker making use of the classic creepy doll theme.

The film was directed by Roland Emmerich, just prior to his big move to Hollywood where he eventually directed blockbusters that included Independence Day, The Patriot and The Day After Tomorrow.

Dolls (1987)

In 1987, Charles Band of Full Moon Features, and Stuart Gordon, of Re-Animator fame, collaborated on what some horror fans consider a ground-breaking film titled simply "Dolls."

This Italian/American film involves six people, caught in a violent thunderstorm, who take refuge in a remote mansion in the English countryside.

The mansion is the home of an elderly couple—Gabriel and Hilary Hartwicke, and their dolls. The Hartwickes we learn, are toymakers. But there's a sinister side to the smiling couple—their dolls are, in reality, instilled with the souls of nasty and cruel people. The Hartwickes we discover, are not just toymakers, but a wizard and witch who have set themselves up as judge, jury and executioners for evil people—all their work is of course carried out by the toys they create.

This underrated film debuted a year before Chucky and made good use of killer toys chasing victims and eliminating them in creative ways.

Child's Play (1988)

Chucky the killer doll has become a horror icon. The first film, Child's Play was made on a budget of 9 million dollars and debuted in November 1988. It was a smash success and grossed more than 44 million dollars, making Chucky a household name.

In the first outing of the series, Chucky, the central figure in the series, is a doll possessed by the soul of an infamous serial killer—Charles Lee "Chucky" Ray, aka the Lakeshore Strangler.

Fatally shot, Ray uses a Haitian Voodoo spell to transfer his soul into a "Good Guy" doll which later ends up in the hands of a widow and her son. As the story unfolds, the killer learns that the longer his soul is trapped in the doll's body, the more human the doll will become. A murderous rampage ensues as Chucky tries to take control of a human boy.

As the film series continued, Chucky became more and more absurd, and the stories delve deeply into dark humor. The series also won a Saturn Award for Best Horror Franchise.

According to writer Don Mancini, the Chucky stories took homage from the Cabbage Patch craze of the 1980s, twisting a wholesome figure (Good Guy dolls in the film) into a nightmare horror icon. The Good Guy doll represented the nostalgic toy every kid had to have. Placed in a horror scenario, it served as a compelling and twisted take on the period's slasher movies.

Many people claim Chucky was also influenced by stories of real life haunted doll, Robert.

Directed and co-written by Tom Holland, from a Don Mancini story, the first film's success led not only to a long series of sequels, but a range of other merchandise including toys, comic books, and replica Chucky dolls. The seventh and latest installment in the series titled Cult of Chucky was released in October 2017. According to industry reports, the franchise, and its resulting merchandise, has generated over $250 million dollars to date.

Puppet Master (1989)

Hot on the heels of the success of the Child's Play film came another movie involving killer dolls, this time, puppets.

Again, it was Charles Band at the helm and the movie proved to be another success for Full Moon Features.

The Puppet Master is a toy maker during the Nazi reign in Europe. Andre Toulon, has a secret way to create life, bringing the puppets in his show alive. When the Nazis try to steal his secret, Toulon kills himself and his puppets are left in limbo.

Fast forward 50 years later, the toys are discovered in an old hotel by a group of psychics and the puppets begin their rampage.

The puppets never spoke in the film, but each demonstrates its own distinct personality, displayed by appearance, tools and actions. Characters in the film include Blade, Jester, Tunneler, Pinhead and Leech Woman.

The film was a big hit and the evil puppets grew into a cult sensation with fans having their own personal favorites among the characters. To date, nine sequels have been released.

Dolly Dearest (1991)

Directed by Maria Lease, and written by Lease, Peter Sutcliffe and Rod Nave, this direct to video movie had a limited theatrical release in the Midwestern United States.

In Mexico, an archaeologist breaks into an ancient Mayan tomb and unleashes "Sanzia," or, Satan, who takes up residence in the Dolly Dearest factory. What unfolds is a combination of killer doll film, possession movie, and basic good versus evil battle as the lead characters attempt to unravel how the demonic forces are controlling their child and the doll she keeps.

Adding to the creepy factor, this film contains not just one animated evil doll, but many, since Sanzia has taken over the factory and is using the dolls to do his dirty work.

Some reviewers dislike the large-scale animations while others say the numerous dolls included make the atmosphere creepier.

Pinocchio's Revenge (1996)

Directed by Kevin Tenney, who also wrote the screenplay, this is one of the many films that came out in the wake of the successful Child's Play series. Another direct to video release, the story centers around a wooden puppet found buried with a murdered boy. The doll is taken by eight-year-old Zoe and soon, strange accidents begin happening. Zoe blames the accidents on the doll, Pinocchio, who she says is trying to protect her.

Although the doll is the centerpiece of the movie, this film is not really a "killer doll" horror movie, but more of a psychological thriller with a child at the middle of the storyline.

May (2002)

"If you can't find a friend, make one."

May is a little girl who is presented with a special doll, Suzie. Suzie is locked inside a glass case for "safekeeping" until the case is broken open by a group of blind children.

The doll in this film isn't overly active but seems to have an influence over the mind of the child. The doll's oddly angled, blue glass eyes and pursed lips give it a creepy appearance.

The movie delves into the emotional world of childhood loneliness and an anxiety-ridden little girl who can't find a way to connect with the people around her. The story's psychological themes with May and her doll Suzie as the focal points make for an uncomfortable, and at times, disturbing film.

Dead Silence (2007)

"Beware the stare of Mary Shaw. She had no children, only dolls. If you see her in your dreams, make sure you never scream, or she'll cut your tongue

out at the seam."

The town of Ravens Fair is haunted by this strange poem. The tale of a woman named Mary Shaw. Mary was obsessed with creating the perfect ventriloquist dummy. She and her doll Billy are the primary focal points of the film, although there are several other dolls in the movie. More than just several in fact, the count of creepy dolls running around in the film sits at 101.

Dead Silence received mixed reviews and the story's attempts at its own mythology fall short, but overall, director James Wan (of the Conjuring franchise) delivers a somewhat entertaining horror movie with tons of creepy dolls running amok.

The Conjuring (2013)

The Conjuring movie franchise is based on the investigations of real life husband and wife paranormal team, Ed and Lorraine Warren. The first installment in the series introduced audiences to Annabelle, one of the world's most haunted dolls. (The real Annabelle is discussed earlier in this book)

While the first Conjuring movie involves the Perron case, the film includes the first big screen appearance of Annabelle and led to the 2014 release of "Annabelle" a prequel to the 2013 story focused on the doll's journey.

Annabelle (2014)

After the massive success of the Conjuring, Wan went on to produce 2014's Annabelle. Inspired by the real story of the haunted doll. The film is set in 1969 when Doctor John Form gives his expectant wife, Mia, a rare, vintage porcelain doll.

The Forms experience a terrifying night when their neighbors are murdered, and the killers invade the Form home. Police officers arrive in time to save the couple, but one of the killers commits suicide while holding the porcelain doll.

The woman, named Annabelle, turns out to be a member of a satanic cult and has transferred her dark soul into the doll. Standard paranormal fare follows with the creepy doll as host of the satanic killer.

While the actual Annabelle is a raggedy Anne doll, the movie version of Annabelle is much more horrifying in appearance. She bears a resemblance to a ventriloquist's dummy, but her face has numerous lines and crevices causing her to look even weirder when lurking in the shadows. The movie doll's creepiness contributed much to the film's success at the box office.

Annabelle has been called "the queen of scary dolls" and the highly effective 2014 movie did a lot to help her solidify the title.

Robert (2015)

This 2015 release is based on the granddaddy of haunted dolls, Key West's famous Robert the Doll.

In the film, a couple's young son, Gene, receives a gift—a vintage doll, from the family's sinister housekeeper Agatha. Chaos soon erupts in the household as strange events begin to unfold. Furniture is vandalized, items are thrown about the home, and maniacal laughter echoes through the rooms.

While Gene's parents try to figure out the source of the activity, the boy blames everything on Robert the Doll.

A sequel, "The Curse of Robert" followed in 2016.

Unfortunately, these low budget horror films do little justice to the real legend of Robert the Doll and most reviewers were disappointed by them.

✓The Boy (2016)

Written by Stacey Menear and directed by William Brent Bell, The Boy is a Chinese-American psychological horror movie.

The story involves an American woman hired by an elderly British couple to be a nanny for their young child. When she arrives at the remote estate, she discovers the "boy" is actually a porcelain doll named Brahms.

The film starts out strong, an interesting blend of killer doll story and haunted house tale. However, many reviewers were disappointed with the turn of the story when it's revealed Brahms is really a living man hiding in secret passages and rooms in the home.

Annabelle: Creation (2017)

Annabelle: Creation, is the fourth installment in the Conjuring series, and the prequel to 2014's Annabelle.

Going back to 1943, we meet dollmaker Samuel Mullins and his wife Esther who are grieving the loss of their seven-year-old daughter Annabelle who was killed in a tragic accident.

A spirit, one they believe to be their daughter, convinces the dollmaker to transfer its essence into one of the craftsman's porcelain dolls. They soon learn they have been tricked by a demonic entity. The Mullins lock the doll, and the entity away where it remains until 1955.

Orphans, taking refuge in the Mullins home, are tricked into releasing the demonic doll. Hell breaks loose. The film moves to 1967 and ties in to the Satanic cult and the woman Annabelle from the previous film.

The use of dolls in horror movies shows no sign of ending. With the resurgence of characters like Chucky, and the wide success of Annabelle, studios are looking for the next supernatural take on creepy toys and paranormal entertainment. The next little horror may be just around the corner. You never know…

Visiting Creepy Dolls

Archive of the Afterlife

The historic town of Moundsville, West Virginia is well known in paranormal circles as home to the infamous West Virginia State Penitentiary, one of the most haunted sites in the Mountain State. But the town is also home to a small, growing museum of interest to paranormal enthusiasts and those with an interest in all things strange.

Tying together history and the paranormal, the museum's mission is stated on its Website:

"The goal of the Archive is to offer an entertaining, but primarily educational experience into the vast and intriguing realm of the paranormal through exhibits of allegedly haunted relics, cursed artifacts, oddities, informational literature and historically significant items."

Founded by paranormal investigator, Steve Hummel, in 2011, the Archive is billed as "The National Museum of the Paranormal." Since establishing the museum, Hummel has worked hard to grow and expand it each year, constantly adding new items to the collection.

Of course, among the odd and historical items there are plenty of dolls. Some of the dolls in the collection include:

Ashen: A small porcelain doll donated to the Archive anonymously. Hummel notes it simply showed up one day in an old cardboard box along with some other dolls. Visitors report odd and uncomfortable feelings when in the doll's presence. The doll also purportedly "speaks" with certain visitors to the Archive.

The Mutilated Effigy Doll: This doll came from a case in McMechen, West Virginia. The tenants in the case reported strange activity including cabinets that opened and closed on their own, and

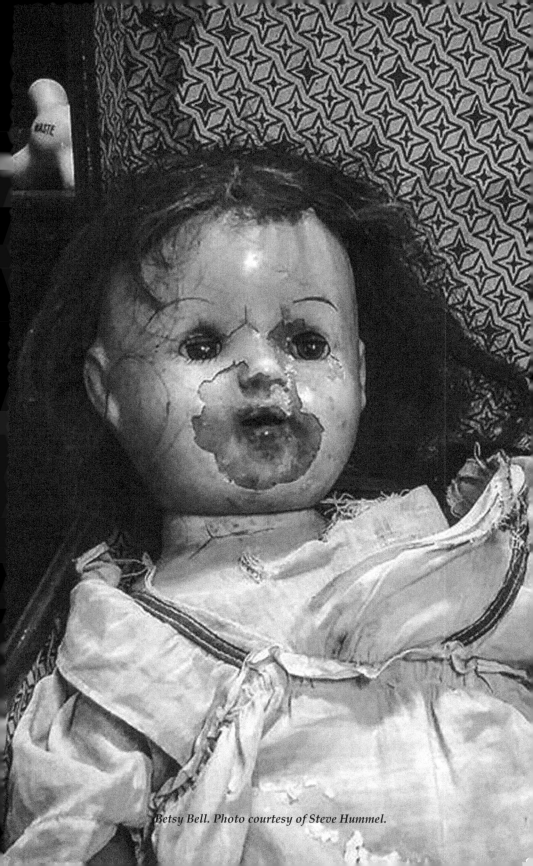

Betsy Bell. Photo courtesy of Steve Hummel.

objects being thrown about. A feeling of being watched persisted in the home, as did a sense of oppression. Once the doll was removed from the property the paranormal activity was reduced. Further investigation of the case is still underway.

Lydia: A doll was purchased by Hummel at an antique shop in West Virginia. Employees at the shop reported strange activity connected to Lydia. Hummel believes there are multiple entities connected to the doll. Visitors to the museum have remarked on the creepy vibe produced by the doll and some have had negative reactions from it:

"On one occasion a lady made the remark that when looking at her (Lydia), she grew very nauseous and immediately walked outside to wait for her friend to finish visiting the museum."

Charlie: A ventriloquist doll removed from a home & business in West Virginia. The doll was terrifying a young boy in the home. Since being placed in the Archive, the doll has moved its head four times. Further investigation is being done on the doll.

Betsy Bell: The doll was donated to the Archive by paranormal investigator Curtis Lee. Lee felt the doll needed to be in the museum and according to the Archive Website states: *"the spirit within the doll is ugly and very well may be demonic."*

Hummel confirms the doll has been blessed but remains one of the darker objects in the museum.

Izzy, Marylin, Jenny, and other dolls fill the small museum. Hummel reports regular activity, and investigators, including Hummel himself and others, have picked up a wide range of evidence at the Archive.

The Archive of the Afterlife is located in the Sanford Center, 1600 3rd St. Second Floor, Ste 202 Moundsville, WV (Corner of third street and Cedar Ave.)

For information on hours and events, see the museum's Website:

https://archive-afterlife.weebly.com/

The Doll Asylum

"We cannot guarantee your safety or mind or spirit, but we will have cookies."

So states the Website for the Doll Asylum, tongue, no doubt, firmly in cheek.

The unusual museum in Oregon is filled with severed doll heads and limbs, a jar of pickled Barbies, countless creepy dolls and even scary clown dolls.

The Doll Asylum is the brainchild of Mark Williams and Heidi Loutzenhiser, a couple from North Portland who started the museum when they moved to the city's Piedmont area in 2010. Originally, the couple decided to host an open house as a way to meet their new neighbors. It was Halloween season, and they wanted a perfect idea. At first, they considered a bird theme, but the plan changed one foggy morning at four A.M. It was when Williams pulled his car out of the drive to make an early airport run that something across the street caught his eye. Leaning against a tree was an oversized doll, creepy in the early morning fog, but inspiring nonetheless. At that moment, the idea for the Doll Asylum came to him.

According to Williams:

"Dolls are perfect, because they're cheap. And they creep people out."

Since the asylum's creation, countless dolls have been added to the collection. Visitors frequently add "macabre" and "demented" looking dolls to the location. Some people simply add dolls without even telling anyone, discreetly placing the new additions on the shelves during their visit.

The event was so successful, the couple decided to invite the public the following year.

Each year, the family spends approximately four weeks staging the various settings. Twenty vignettes fill out the space and creepiness is in abundance.

"It started with just some family friends coming over, now we're on the internet. I just love seeing how they react to the little things we do out and about…it just makes me happy."

The museum's Website spins a background story about a German doctor who founded the Doll Asylum:

"Welcome to the Doll Asylum. We are a place for the old, the decrepit, the forgotten…the insane. We try to 'fix' those we can, and provide a place of refuge for those we can't."

"Founded in 1867 by German Dr. Hermann Reinhardt, the Doll Asylum's purpose was to receive dolls who were abandoned, neglected, or most importantly, showing signs of psychotic or murderous behavior.

Doll maker by hobby, Dr. Reinhardt thought he could bridge the gap between the inanimate and animate and stomp out the dark thoughts that lay beneath.

While no true success was to be had in his day, Dr. Reinhardt did establish a home for those unwanted creatures and in doing so, has protected society at large."

A reporter from station KOIN who visited the Doll Asylums stated:

"I didn't really know what to expect upon arriving to the home that has a hundred or so dolls dwelling inside. What I found was a family who absolutely loves Halloween…and they love celebrating it with everyone."

After the initial 75 dolls, the collection quickly grew. By 2012, the couple had amassed more than 700 dolls, and by 2015, the collection passed the one thousand doll mark.

In 2017, the Doll Asylum relocated to Astoria, Oregon with a current, and still growing collection, of over 1,300 dolls. Williams notes:

"All of these are donated or brought from Goodwill or other thrift shops. All, that is, but the first seventy-five. Those were left to Loutzenhiser when her mother died."

The Oregonian newspaper featured the Dolly Asylum in a 2015 article, calling it one of the five ways to celebrate Halloween in the area. Reporter Michael Lloyd noted that the museum was "creepy but fun."

"North Portland's Doll Asylum is a truly creepy Halloween experience. Breaking the mold from the haunted house thrills, the makeshift doll-themed museum displays old dolls in vast numbers around a house—creepy enough

in their own right."

The asylum is free and open to the public each year around Halloween. Visitors can enjoy a free cup of coffee or cider while touring the macabre scenes of the Doll Asylum. Donations are welcomed, and proceeds are given to the Brody Borlaug Foundation at Doernbecher Children's Hospital.

Note that some of the scenes at the asylum may be too disturbing for young children.

Find out more information about the museum at their Website:

www.Dollasylum.com

The Enchanted Doll Forest

"Anyone that needs a home for unwanted or broken dolls, please bring them here."

Shirley Kraus Mancuso, along with her business partner, Eleanor McBride, have funneled their passion for dolls into the creation of a unique place, the Enchanted Doll Forest. The "forest" is actually an antique store and consignment shop located in Cortlandt Manor in the town of Cortlandt, northern Westchester County, New York. The shop also bills itself as a "doll and teddy bear hospital," and it attracts collectors and curiosity seekers from far and wide. Mancuso is adamant she will accept any unwanted dolls regardless of their condition:

"They would end up in a landfill and that is just a piece of history getting thrown out. Even Barbie dolls, bring them here, they would just stay in a landfill forever."

At the shop's initial opening, it included about two thousand items, mostly dolls. There are a wide range of dolls, from inexpensive ones that can be had for as little as ten dollars, to expensive antiques that hit prices over a thousand dollars each.

"When I get a bargain, I give a bargain," states Mancuso.

There are antique bisque dolls that date back to the 1850s and as late as the 1920s. These popular collectibles from the mid-19th century are unique and highly desired by doll collectors.

177

The shop also has doll houses that Mancuso makes herself. Those too are on display in the store. She makes custom orders and specialty items. The younger generations, she says, like "weird stuff."

Mancuso is a native of the Putnam Valley and says she's had a passion for "dolls, teddy bears and cutesy stuff" her whole life.

"I guess I never grew up, and my parents never said no," she states.

Mancuso went to nursing school, but her passion for dolls drew her back towards the field of doll collecting and history. She ended up working at flower shops while learning the trade of dolls. She has worked through the Yorktown museum for years, teaching doll making and history classes. It's her passion that led her to open the Enchanted Doll forest. She loves dealing with the dolls and meeting other collectors.

For those with a phobia of dolls, the shop is not a place to spend time. Thousands of doll faces stare out, watching each visitor. In some cases, there are only the heads of dolls with improvised bodies made of newspaper and dressed in period appropriate clothing. Mancuso says she turns no doll away, even if it's only a piece of a doll.

Due perhaps to her willingness to take in any doll, in short order, Mancuso found her shop a center of paranormal activity.

Initially the incidents were "minor" with lights turning off and on, items being moved about, etc...but it wasn't long before the activity increased. Mancuso started hearing her name being called when no one was there. The shop's radio would turn itself off and on and there was a constant sense of "not being alone" even when there was no one else in the store.

Mancuso began to keep a journal of all the activity and decided to contact local paranormal teams in the hope they could get to the bottom of things and perhaps offer some solutions.

Unfortunately, the investigations only stirred things up more. Patterns started to form amidst the activity. Mancuso would open the shop some mornings to find certain dolls scattered around the shop, or in piles on the floor in the center of the store. She was haunted by the sound of breaking glass and began to hear disembodied laughter behind her.

As the activity continued to build, Mancuso noted that two newly acquired dolls were crying by themselves. She witnessed other dolls fly across the shop. Random piles of dolls became more frequent. Others would be ripped off the walls from their displays and thrown on the floor, and the strange sounds increased.

In the midst of it all, Mancuso learned there was a distinct market for haunted dolls. She would inform people about the activity demonstrated by items she believed were haunted, and many people expressed an interest in learning about her own experiences. But dealing with the haunted items became too much for her on a personal level.

She quit openly dealing with haunted items, at least knowingly, and downsized her shop. The haunted items, she believes, ruined her business and she tells people it's best to leave such things alone:

"I don't recommend haunted things to anyone—and be prepared to deal with THINGS afterwards."

From Victorian dolls to Tim Burton styled dollhouses, from Native American dolls to presidential dolls, modern to antique, there's a little something for every doll collector at the Enchanted Doll Forest—and something to be disturbed by for those with a fear of dolls.

Update—The Enchanted Doll Forest has relocated to Putnam Valley, New York. They still sell a wide range of dolls and collectibles. Visit them on the Web for further information:

https://www.manta.com/c/mxjknnj/enchanted-doll-forest

The Island of the Dolls (La Isla de las Muñecas)

A journey to the Island of the Dolls is not an easy task. The island is located almost twenty miles south of the center of Mexico City, far from the urban sprawl of the huge metropolis, in a rich farmland steeped in tradition and superstition. The island is in the Xochimilco borough, (pronounced: so-chee-mel-koh) a region crisscrossed by a large network of canals. These canals are the last remnants of an ancient body of water known as Lake Xochimilco.

To navigate the canals of Xochimilco, it is necessary to hire a tranjinera. Tranjineras are brightly colored wooden boats propelled by the use of a long pole, much like the famous gondolas of Venice.

The trip to the Island of the Dolls from Mexico City takes about two hours each way by boat. There are few natives who speak English in this region, so it is important that you are able to make the boat's pilot understand that you want to go to "La Isla de las Muñecas", otherwise you could end up on a basic tour around the canals.

Additionally, in recent years, another issue has arisen. There are now several other "islands of dolls" created by industrious residents attempting to cash in on tourists looking for the unusual original. These newer locations are usually a much shorter journey and have nowhere near the number of dolls as the real La Isla de las Muñecas. Purportedly, one site has even replicated the shack on the original island in an attempt to fool sharp eyed seekers. The best advice for finding the real site is to either connect with a trusted local who can get you there, or to find the coordinates to the real island and correlate them on your journey.

And don't forget to pick up a doll and some offerings before the trip, otherwise you may anger whatever spirits call this strange little place home.

The John Zaffis Museum of the Paranormal

Sitting in a separate building behind his private residence, John Zaffis' museum is home to a collection gathered over many years of paranormal investigation.

Zaffis is a well-known figure in the field, from his involvement with the "Haunting in Connecticut" case, to his popular reality show, The Haunted Collector. John's main focus over the years has been cases involving haunted objects.

The museum includes a large number of dolls, including Simon, a haunted ventriloquist doll, a pair of marionettes believed to have spiritual energy, and Mr. Bojo, an antique poppet that caused terrible nightmares for its previous owner.

When John gets new acquisitions, he goes through a procedure to "neutralize" the haunted item before putting it in place. After John's process, the item is placed in a large barn that houses the collection. But even after the binding rituals are completed, it doesn't mean the item is completely clear and safe.

As John states:

"You have a building filled with a tremendous amount of items, therefore, you're always going to have that energy within. There's no guarantee that the energy associated with an item is going to be totally gone after some binding rituals...you're always going to have paranormal activity regardless of the different things that occur or happen."

On occasion, Zaffis has let other investigators in the museum. Independent people have captured EVPs (electronic voice phenomena) and anomalous things in photographs.

At this time, the museum is on private property and not open to the public. John is working on relocating the collection to a public setting where it can be accessible to visitors. His goal is for people to be able to see the items, but of course, they won't be able to touch any of the objects since the items are considered dangerous.

Some items in the Zaffis museum have been chronicled in two books written by John and co-author Rosemary Ellen Guiley: "Haunted by the things you Love" and "Demon Haunted."

Check John's Website for further information and updates:

https://www.johnzaffis.com/museum

Pollock's Toy Museum

Number 1 Scala Street, London, is a short walk from Oxford Street and not far from London's famous Underground. Here lies a dimly lit Victorian building, a pair of townhouses joined together to form a museum. At first, the location appears small, but inside, one discovers a winding maze. Wooden floors, low ceilings, small rooms—and toys. Lots and lots of toys. This is Pollock's Toy Museum.

Named one of London's best small museums, Pollock's is named after Benjamin Pollock, one of the last printers in the toy theatre trade, a popular pastime of the1800s. The museum itself was created during the 1950s by Marguerite Fawdry. In the late 1960s, Pollock's moved to its current location where it remains to this day. The museum is an independent, family run business built up over the years by purchases and donations from friends, family and the public.

Pollock's has been described as: *"A creaking Dickensian warren"*.

The museum is a step back in time to a period before computers, iPads, and mobile phones. It contains a wide-ranging collection of antique toys, from vintage board games to a collection of teddy bears. There are toys made from plastic, lead, tin and wood. There's even a mouse fashioned from Nile clay that's purportedly 4,000 years old.

And then, there are the dolls.

Wooden dolls from the Netherlands, Asian dolls in traditional dress, hundred-and-fifty-year-old Victorian dolls. Plastic dolls, dolls with porcelain faces, rare dolls with wax heads, ragdolls with tangles of hair, and some that are bald.

Glass eyes stare out from porcelain faces, some wide-eyed, others small and creepy. There are dolls with happy expressions and dolls with sour faces.

An entire room filled with dolls.

The room has a glassed-off area with vintage, wrought iron beds and model carriages with dolls in 19th century clothing. It's the last room on the museum's tour before the exit and many visitors can't handle spending time in the room. Some, in fact, backtrack all the way to the front of the museum rather than going through the doll room to exit.

"The dolls creep me out," stated one woman. "I took a single step into the room, and that was enough. I went back out all the way through to the front."

Museum employee, Ken Hoyt, says many people get "freaked out" by the room. Most often, it's adults that can't deal with the dolls. Hoyt adds, it's more frequent for people to get frightened or nervous during the winter months when the sun goes down early, and the rooms are a bit darker.

"It's like you'd think they've gone through a haunted house...It's not a great way to end their visit to the Pollock's Toy Museum, because anything else that they would have seen that would have been charming and wonderful is totally gone now."

Hoyt adds that people often come out saying they hated the last room because of all the dolls and the creepy feeling of "so many eyes" watching them. The dolls people find the most unsettling at Pollock's are the ones that bear an eerie resemblance to humans but have started to decay due to age:

"...the dolls that people find particularly creepy are the ones that look more lifelike...these are the ones that have begun to decay in eerily inhuman ways. The dolls don't age well...I think any time that a doll really tried to look like a human being and now is 100 years old, the hair is decaying, the eyes don't work anymore. So, it looks as much like a baby as possible, but like an ancient baby."

Some people state the "Creepy Doll Room" is the downside to Pollocks, calling it "nightmare inducing." It certainly is for anyone who suffers from pediophobia, but even those who don't have such a fear find themselves unnerved when walking through the doll room. Hoyt says many people come out of the room making statements blended with nervous laughter. Comments about how much they hate dolls and can't look at them. Hoyt believes that dolls:

"...don't really frighten people so much as they "creep" them out."

Ironically, there's a frequent concern that the antique toys may be too much for small children. Even the museum's Website stipulates:

"Please do come and visit the museum. We recommend it for slightly older children and adults of all ages."

Some people have reported strange experiences around the dolls and believe that some of the items at least, are haunted. One visitor noted:

"When we went in that room, my girlfriend said she felt like there were spirits in there with us. I don't really subscribe to that kind of notion, but something just wasn't right. It just wasn't right in that room.

There's one sinister looking doll back there. I swear when we were in there, that doll moved. Just a slight turn of its head, as if it turned to watch us better. I was never afraid of dolls before, but after being in there, I can't stand them anymore."

Other visitors have stated they've heard anomalous sounds and even unexplained voices in the doll room.

"...there's something in there, something alive. I think at least one of those dolls is possessed or has a spirt attached to it. My sister and I heard a disembodied voice when we were in that room. It was too much for us, we got out of there as quick as we could."

183

The museum has become a curious stop for those who want to explore its dusty shelves, winding rooms and countless, vintage toys. Some come just to test themselves in the creepy doll room, and perhaps, catch some movement in a room full of human-appearing non-human objects.

Pollock's Toy Museum and shop is located in London's Fitzrovia at: 1 Scala St., Fitzrovia, London, UK. For more information, check their Website at:

http://pollockstoys.com/

Spooked in Seattle

Located in downtown Seattle's Pioneer Square, Spooked in Seattle has been running ghost tours of the city since 2004. In association with AGHOST (Advanced Ghost Hunters of Seattle), the tours relate the real hauntings of the city, along with evidence collected during investigations.

The company offers a number of tours, including a history tour and ghost hunting events. Spooked in Seattle's storefront is below street level and is part of Seattle's famous underground. It's also the starting point of the company's tours.

The Seattle headquarters houses both a gift shop, and the Seattle Death Museum featuring historic items collected over the years by Spooked founder Ross Allison.

One of Allison's other passions has been collecting haunted items which are also on display at Spooked in Seattle. Among the items in the collection are around thirty haunted dolls, including "Mr. Creepy," the haunted ventriloquist doll featured in this book.

Spooked in Seattle has been featured in various news media including CNN and ABC's NightLine.

New items and dolls are being added all the time, and the storefront is a must see stop when visiting Seattle.

Spooked in Seattle is located at 102 Cherry St. Seattle, WA 98104. For further information including hours and tour costs, check the

Website:

http://spookedinseattle.squarespace.com/

Tom Devlin's Monster Museum

Tom Devlin loves monsters. Since 2001, he's worked in the field of makeup and special effects. But it's not just a job for Tom, it's his passion. His company 1313FX has provided creatures and makeup effects for over a hundred feature films.

Devlin became a fan favorite after appearing on SyFy's makeup themed contest show, "Face Off." Following his passion for monsters, Devlin decided to open a museum to highlight his collection.

Devlin also hopes to educate the public in the art he loves so much. Since the success of Face Off, the industry has new life and more people are interested in working in the field.

Tom Devlin's Monster Museum. Photo by author.

As the museum's Website states:

"Our mission is to preserve the art and history of special makeup effects. This gallery of Tom's art includes everything from screen used props and creature suits to custom pieces representing monsters throughout movie history."

Tom has worked on over a hundred films to date and has traveled around the country for gigs. His museum reflects the range of his interest in monsters. Devlin already has plans to expand the museum further, pointing to the additional one thousand square feet behind the wall of its current location.

Located in historic Boulder City, Nevada, between Las Vegas and the Hoover Dam, one of the highlights currently at the museum is the special Puppet Master display, including screen used props and dolls from the series. There's also props from Chucky and other doll related horror films.

Tom Devlin's Monster Museum is located at 1310 Nevada Hwy, Boulder City, NV. For hours and ticket information, check the museum's Website:

http://tomdevlinsmonstermuseum.com/

The Warren's Occult Museum

In a quiet area of Connecticut is one of the world's largest collections of haunted objects. The Warren's Occult Museum was founded by Ed and Lorraine Warren and is home to the collection of haunted and possessed items they amassed over their years investigating reports of paranormal activity around the world.

Lorraine, a trance medium, and her late husband Ed, a demonologist, formed NESPR (The New England Centre for Psychic Research) in 1952. The Warrens have become popular in recent years since their cases inspired the successful film franchise "The Conjuring" series.

The museum has numerous dolls, including "The Shadow Doll." The Shadow Doll has been called an "extremely dangerous object," and was purportedly used as a vessel to inflict pain and suffering on victims. Reportedly, the doll's sole purpose is to create misery and negativity.

However, Lorraine believes the "worst item" in the museum is the haunted doll Annabelle. It's also the most famous item in the occult collection. Annabelle has inspired a pair of successful films that put the doll in the spotlight, but it's history is much older than the recent movies. Annabelle has been through several exorcisms, yet it's believed negative energy remains attached to the doll.

Tony Spera now runs NESPR and oversees the museum's collection. On occasion, the organization hosts special events called "An Evening With Annabelle." The evening includes a lecture, a review of NESPR cases, a banquet, and of course, a chance to see the real Annabelle. The doll is of course safely sealed away in a glass and wooden case with spiritual protections and blessings to keep any potential negative energy encased within the doll.

According to the Website, the occult museum is currently closed due to zoning regulations. Spera and his team are looking for a new location for the collection and hope to have it accessible to the public soon. In the meantime, check the Website for updates and for event announcements:

http://www.warrens.net/Occult-Museum-Tours.html

Yesterday's Children
Antique Doll & Toy Museum

"Two Centuries of Wonder seen through a child's eyes!"

"The Wonder of Childhood, children and toys, captured in over 1,000 dolls dating back to 1843 in an historic setting."

For twenty-eight years, Carolyn Bakarich operated a small museum in the downtown historic district of Vicksburg, Mississippi.

"Yesterday's Children Antique Doll & Toy Museum" opened in 1986. It's filled with more than a thousand dolls including an extensive collection of rare, late Victorian era dolls produced by famous doll makers such as Simon & Halbig of Germany, and Jumeau of France.

Carolyn's husband, Mike, says the collection was at their home for some time before the museum opened:

"At one time, they were all at home. They were in all the rooms. I told her to do something, so I could have a place to sit."

"She was a collector. My son-in-law said if she lived in the Sahara Desert, her yard would have more sand than anyone else's."

The museum is bursting with toys, every room and hall filled to the brim. There's a featured collection of boy's toys with G.I. Joes, and an extensive toy car collection. And of course, there are dolls. From every era and region, they fill the shelves, walls, even the floors. Eyes seem to peer out from every single nook and corner of the museum. A nightmare place to be locked in for those with a fear of dolls and their human-like eyes and other features.

Bakarich says his wife opened the museum because of her love of the toys she had collected:

"Because she wanted to share her collection with the public. She wanted other people to enjoy it. Women would come in, and they would talk about the dolls. She knew the histories of the dolls and would love to talk with people about them."

Carolyn Bakarich passed away in October 2014 due to complications from a fall she had suffered in 2013.

The woman was well loved by the community of Vicksburg and her passing was felt by many. As the executive director of the Vicksburg Convention and Visitors Bureau noted:

"We're heartbroken at the loss of Miss B. She had a beautiful collection, and the museum was so much a part of the city's downtown. I hope the family can do something to keep it here, because we want the museum to stay in Vicksburg."

"If it is possible, I'd like to see if I can help them, so we can keep the museum here. It's an asset to the community and a different attraction from the other things we have here, and Vicksburg needs attractions."

The museum's Website states:

"Collectors, children, and doll and toy enthusiasts will revel in the magnificent and extensive displays of dolls and toys of the 19th and 20th century."

Self-guided tours are available, so visitors can take their time looking over the vast collection. There's also a gift shop on site filled with nostalgic toys and civil war gifts.

Carolyn opened the museum when she and her husband moved to Vicksburg. In 1986, the location was in a building on Washington Street, but in 1987, it moved to its current location in the downtown historic district. The museum became a "must see stop" for many visitors to the area's historic downtown. According to Mike, the number of visitors varied according to the season.

"Sometimes when the American Queen visited here, it would be people from the boat. We had more visitors in summer and spring than in the fall."

Mike Bakarich reports that after his wife's passing, several auction houses called him asking about possible purchase of the collection. Mike considered the idea and the museum's future was up in the air for a time. The Bakarich children live in different areas of the country. Although they visit Vicksburg often, none of them moved to take over the site's operation.

"I'm not sure if any of them feel they are ready to take over the museum."

Mike, a retired brigadier general has continued running the museum since Carolyn passed away, unable to part with something that was so important to his wife.

In 2017, Ghost Adventures aired an episode featuring their investigation of the Doll Museum. During the show, Mike told team lead Zak Bagans the collection currently contains 1,851 dolls, not counting those for sale in the gift shop. Zak asked Mike for some details about the museum:

Zak asked,*"Do you ever feel that your wife visits the dolls?"*

Mike replied *"Always, her spirit is here, they meant a lot to her."*

Before her death, Carolyn told her husband about one particular doll with connections to the Holocaust. The doll is purported to have the spirit of a little girl attached to it. According to Mike's account, the family shipped the doll to the states as the Nazis rolled through Europe rounding up Jewish people:

"Before the Germans picked them up and moved them to a concentration camp, to placate the little girl, the parents packaged the doll and shipped it to safety in the United States.

Her owner thought the world of this doll and took steps to have the doll safeguarded and in turn was not safeguarded and perished."

The doll was produced in 1920 by German doll makers Koenig & Wernicke, a toy company active from 1911-1935. The museum obtained the doll from a family estate sale.

The doll is reported to be active and is known to move of its own accord. People have also sensed a little girl attached to the doll.

Despite his fear of dolls, Zak investigated the museum by himself, setting the German doll on a chair with a camera facing it. He also placed a recorder in front of the doll's mouth. During the investigation, a loud "hiss" was captured, seemingly coming from the doll.

As the investigation continued, a toy mobile started to move on its own. Zak sat down on the floor in hopes of being closer to any potential child spirits that could be present.

While he was seated on the floor, a doll at the far end of the aisle suddenly fell off one of the upper shelves. Upon investigation, the doll proved to be a small figure labeled "Miss Revlon" from 1958. Interestingly, the incident occurred near the chair where Zak had placed the haunted holocaust doll.

Zak called in Jay and the two used a Mel meter to check EMF readings on the doll that moved. The investigators observed and recorded as the EMF readings rose all the way to 1.1 on the meter. Additionally, Zak and Jay felt what they described as an "ice cold energy mass" near the doll.

A curious follow up to the investigation occurred when the episode aired on live television. Sharp eyed viewers caught what appears to be the manifestation of a small hand moving behind Zak amid the shelves of dolls. No one else was present in the museum during the segment and certainly not any living children.

What ghosts lurk in this historic Vicksburg museum? According to her husband, the former owner's spirit still visits her beloved dolls, but perhaps there are other souls too, attached and/or attracted to the mass of dolls filling this curious spot in the old south.

The museum is located at: 1104 Washington St. Vicksburg, Mississippi. For more information, including hours and visiting information, check the museum's Website:

http://www.yesterdayschildrenmuseum.com/

Zak Bagans' The Haunted Museum

"It looks like the Winchester Mystery House."

"I love this place. I don't like being away from it when I'm filming. It was meant for me to have this place. I'm feeling like Sarah Winchester a little bit—I'll never stop building and adding little things."

So stated Zak Bagans' in an interview about his new haunted museum. Located in a historic section of Las Vegas, Nevada, the museum is the latest endeavor by well-known host, and lead investigator of the Travel Channel's popular show, Ghost Adventures.

Bagans' searched for a location in Vegas for eight years before finding the historic mansion and purchasing it in 2015. The home is an 11,000-square foot Tudor revival building with a peaked roof and multi-paned windows. It was constructed in 1938 by the wealthy businessman Cyril Wengert.

The mansion itself has a supernatural history including the purported presence of spirits and a basement once used for Satanic rituals. All of course—before Zak moved in with his haunted collection.

Bagans' started collecting curios and haunted antiques when he was a kid and has continued through the years, amassing an amazing collection that he has now installed in his Vegas museum. As he states:

"Think of objects—dolls, books, utensils, just about anything—as sponges that can soak up the energy and emotions of people around them. Those emotions are absorbed into these objects, and sometimes a spirit will attach itself to those objects."

"The whole experience for people to come in here, it's about mystery, it's about the thrill of wondering whether or not you're going to have an experience with something supernatural."

After working on the exhibits for almost two years, the Haunted Museum opened in the fall of 2017.

There are numerous haunted dolls in Zak's museum, a large display showcases ventriloquist dolls, puppets and a wide range of dolls from across the ages.

Zak's Museum is also home to the infamous Peggy, one of the world's most haunted dolls. Because of the intensity of the reports, Peggy has her own room at the museum.

Zak Bagans' Haunted Museum, Las Vegas, NV. Photo by author.

According to the museum's Website:

"Paranormal enthusiasts visiting Zak Bagans' The Haunted Museum will venture down creepy, winding hallways and secret passages into more than 30 rooms that rival scenes from Hollywood horror films, setting the stage for frightening facts about each paranormal piece...In every room I want you to experience different energy, different emotions."

Zak Bagans' The Haunted Museum is located at 600 E. Charleston Blvd, Las Vegas, NV. Tickets are available online and at the museum's ticket office. Due to the nature of the exhibits, children under the age of 16 are not permitted. For more details, as well as information on special events, check the Website at:

https://thehauntedmuseum.com/

Bibliography

Alvarado, Denise. Voodoo Dolls in Magick and Ritual. CreateSpace Independent Publishing, 2009.

Bromage, Bernard. Occult Arts of Ancient Egypt. HarperCollins Publishing, New York, New York, 1971.

Cavendish, Marshall. Man, Myth & Magic: An Illustrated Encyclopedia of the Supernatural, Part 50. Marshall Cavendish Corp, 1970.

Crowley, Aleister. Moonchild. Red Wheel/Weiser, Newburyport, Massachusetts, 1971.

Epton, Nina. The Palace and the Jungle. Oldbourne Press, London, England, 1960.

Fox, Carl, and Landshoff, H. The Doll New Shorter Edition. New York, New York, Harry N. Abrams, Inc. 1973.

Frazer, James George. The Golden Bough. Macmillian Publishing, London, England. 1951.

Freud, Sigmund. The Uncanny. Penguin Classics, Penguin Publishing, London, England, 2003.

Gaskill, Malcolm. Witchcraft in England, 1560-1760. Palgrave Macmillian, London, England, 1997.

Graham, Stacey. Haunted Stuff Demonic Dolls, Screaming Skulls & Other Creepy Collectibles. Woodbury, Minnesota, Llewellyn Publications, 2014.

Gray, WG. Magical Ritual Methods. Red Wheel/Weiser, Newburyport, Massachusetts, 1980.

Harker, John. Demonic Dolls True Tales of Terrible Toys. CreateSpace Independent Publishing, 2015.

Harris, Jayne. Peggy the Doll. CreateSpace Independent Publishing, 2017

King, Constance Eileen. The Collector's History of Dolls. New York, New York, Bonanza Books, 1977.

McAndrew, Francis T. & Koehnke, Sara S. On the Nature of Creepiness. New Ideas in Psychology, Department of Psychology, Knox College, Galesburg, IL. 2016.

Mori, Masahiro (Bukimi No Tani) Valley of Eeriness. Independent research paper, 1970.

Okonowicz, Ed. Possessed Possessions. Elkton, Maryland. Myst and Lace Publishers, 1996.

Phillips, Perrott, Editor. Out Of This World The Illustrated Library of the Bizarre and Extraordinary, Volume 23. Phoebus Publishing Company/BPC Publishing, Paulton, England, 1976.

Quinata, Anthony. Harold the Doll. CreateSpace Independent Publishing, 2015.

Reichardt, Jasia. Robots: Fact, Fiction, and Prediction. Penguin Books, London, England, 1978.

Robertson, A.F. Life Like Dolls: The Collector Doll Phenomenon and the Lives of Women Who Love Them. Routledge, London, England, 2003.

Schmidt, Leigh Eric. From Demon Possession to Magic Show: Ventriloquism, Religion, and the Enlightenment. Church History, Volume 67, No 2. Cambridge University Press New York, New York, 1998.

Sloan, David, Robert the Doll. Phantom Press, Key West, Florida, 2014.

Smith, Barbara. Ghost Stories and Mysterious Creatures of British Columbia. Lone Pine Publishing, Edmonton, Alberta, Canada, 1999.

Tralins, Robert. Children of the Supernatural. Lancer Books, New York, NY, 1969.

Vox, Valentine. I Can See Your Lips Moving, The History and Art of Ventriloquism. Plato Publishing / Empire Publications, Manchester, England. 1993.

Zaffis, John, and Guiley, Rosemary Ellen, Haunted by the things you love. Visionary Living Inc, New Milford, CT. 2014

Internet Resources

Hayley is a Ghost blog

http://hayleyisaghost.co.uk/

Sex Gore Mutants

http://www.sexgoremutants.co.uk/frame1.html

Vice UK Website

https://www.vice.com/en_uk

About the Author

David Weatherly is a renaissance man of the strange and supernatural. He has traveled the world in pursuit of ghosts, cryptids, UFOs, magic, and more. From the specters of dusty castles, to remote, haunted islands, from ancient sites, to modern mysteries, he has journeyed to the most unusual places on the globe seeking the unknown.

David became fascinated with the paranormal at a young age. Ghost stories and accounts of weird creatures and UFOs led him to discover many of his early influences. Writers such as such as John Keel, Jacques Vallee, Hans Holzer and others set him on course to spend his life exploring and investigating the unexplained.

Throughout his life, he's also delved into shamanic and magical traditions from around the world, spending time with elders from numerous cultures in Europe, the Americas, Africa and Asia. He has studied with Taoist masters in China, Tibetan Lamas, and other mystics from the far east. He's picked up knowledge from African and Native American tribal elders and sat around fires with shaman from countless other traditions.

Along his path, David has also gathered a lot of arcane knowledge, studying a range of ancient arts from palmistry, the runes, and other obscure forms of divination, to alchemy and magick. He has studied and taught Qigong and Ninjutsu, as well as various energy related arts. David has also studied stage and performance magic.

His shamanic and magical background has given him a unique perspective in his explorations into the unknown, and he continues to write, travel and explore, leaving no stone unturned in his quest for the strange and unusual.

David has investigated, and written about, a diverse range of topics including, Hauntings & Ghosts, Cryptozoology, Ufology, Ancient Mysteries, Shamanism, Magic and Psychic Phenomena.

In 2012, David founded the independent media and publishing company, Leprechaun Productions.

He has been a featured speaker at conferences around the world and has lectured for countless paranormal and spiritual groups.

He is a frequent guest on Coast to Coast AM with George Noory, Spaced Out Radio and other radio programs. David has also appeared on numerous television shows including the Travel Channel's Mysteries of the Outdoors, History Channel's Ancient Aliens, Beyond Belief and other programs.

David's books include Strange Intruders, Black Eyed Children and the "Haunted" series.

To find David online:

http://www.eerielights.com

Made in the USA
Columbia, SC
25 November 2020